A GIFT TO EVERY FRESH GRADUATE

27 Essential Skills Not Taught in School

SEGUN ESHO

A GIFT TO EVERY FRESH GRADUATE – 27 SKILLS NOT TAUGHT IN SCHOOL © 2023. **Segun Esho.**

All rights reserved. No part of this book may be reproduced by any mechanical, photographic, or electronic process, or in the form of a phonographic recording; nor may it be stored in a retrieval system, transmitted, or otherwise be copied for public or private use—other than for "fair use" as brief quotations embodied in articles and reviews—without prior written permission of the publisher. This publication is designed to provide accurate and authoritative information regarding the subject matter covered. It is sold with the understanding that the publisher is not engaged in rendering legal, accounting, or other professional services. If you require legal advice or other expert assistance, you should seek the services of a competent professional.

Work and dedication are essential components of success. The outcomes and case studies that are provided in this book are the results that were achieved by direct collaboration with the book's author. When practicing any of the fundamental skills listed in this book, you should keep in mind that your outcomes may differ.

Segun Esho © 2023– All Rights Reserved.

ACKNOWLEDGEMENTS

A book is never written alone, and "27 Essential Skills Not Taught in School - A Gift to Every Fresh Graduate" was no exception. I would like to take this opportunity to thank everyone who contributed to the publication of this book.

First and foremost, I would like to thank my amiable wife Temitope Esho and lovely children Toni, Esther and Damilola for their unwavering support and encouragement throughout the writing process. Their love and support have been the foundation upon which everything else is built. Their understanding kept me going even when the going got tough.

I also want to express my gratitude to my team of editors, proofreaders and publishers – Precious Onome, Seun Adebowale, Nnamdi Adonis, Tobi Olaniyi, Tunji Adeboyejo, Seth A. Thomas for their invaluable contributions to the book. Their attention to detail and commitment to excellence helped make this book the best it could be.

To my students, colleagues, mentors, and friends who have provided me with insight and feedback, I am deeply grateful. Your expertise and support have been instrumental in the creation of this book.

ACKNOWLEDGEMENTS

Finally, I would like to thank the readers of this book for their support and enthusiasm. It is my sincere hope that the strategies and advice offered within these pages will help you achieve success in your personal and professional lives.

Thank you all.

Segun Esho

Table of Contents

Acknowledgements	3
Table Of Contents	5
Introduction	7
Skil 1: Communication Skills	10
Skil 2: Interpersonal Skills	16
Skil 3: Networking/Socialising Skills	22
Skil 4: Organisational Skills	28
Skil 5: Goal Setting Skills	34
Skil 6: Problem Solving Skills	43
Skil 7: Decision-Making Skills	49
Skil 8: Leadership Skills	55
Skil 9: Business Writing Skills	61
Skil 10: Negotiation Skills	70

Table of Contents

Skil 11: Selling Skills — **76**

Skil 12: Entrepreneurial Skills — **82**

Skil 13: Team Building Skills — **89**

Skil 14: Cv/Resume Writing Skills — **95**

Skil 15: Business Plan Writing Skills — **103**

Skil 16: Time Management Skills — **114**

Skil 17: Emotional Intelligence Skills — **120**

Skil 18: Creativity And Innovation Skill — **126**

Skil 19: Social Media/Digital Marketing Skill — **133**

Skil 20: Personal Financial Management Skill — **141**

Skil 21: Speed Reading Skills — **147**

Skil 22: Simple Etiquette Skills — **155**

Skil 23: Safety And Security Skills — **160**

Skil 24: Public Speaking Skills — **167**

Skil 25: Job Interviewing Skills — **176**

Skil 26: Stress Management Skills — **181**

Skil 27: Work-Life Balance Skills — **187**

Conclusion — **193**

INTRODUCTION

Congratulations on graduating and making it out of the four walls of the university. Welcome to the real world. If you're reading this, you are most likely a fresh graduate, which is the time of your life you've always talked about. You probably did not prepare for the fears and uncertainties you're facing right now. No worries, you'll eventually get along. I'd like you to know that you are lucky to have this book in your hand right now, as it will help you navigate the uncertainties.

Now that you've gotten the degree you've always dreamt about, what next? You probably realize now that there are thousands, if not tens of thousands, of other fresh graduates like you. How do you stand out? What are your chances of getting that dream job seeing as almost every graduate seems qualified? Here is a little gift from me containing relevant and sort-after soft skills that will help increase your chances of getting hired, irrespective of the high stakes.

Soft skills are becoming increasingly important, but there's not enough information about them. Soft skills are essential skills that you can't necessarily teach in a classroom. It seems impossible to know when to use soft skills or how to develop them in the first place. Research has shown that soft skills are often the most predictive of job performance. These are skills that are difficult to teach but can have an enormous impact on your career growth.

In this journey, we will explore how you can develop and polish your soft skills over time to increase your performance. The first step is understanding your strengths and weaknesses to determine where to focus your efforts. Secondly, you should develop a growth mindset that will allow you to learn from failures and mistakes to strengthen your soft skills. Thirdly, you must take care of yourself by practicing self-compassion and self-care and ensuring adequate sleep and exercise. Finally, you need to find a support system or mentor who will help guide you through this process of building your soft skills - someone with experience with these skills that they can share with you.

These essential skills make up the in-between, more difficult skills to measure and quantify. Typically, these skills are learned on the job or from previous work experience. There are hundreds of different types of Soft Skills, but there are some common skills that all people use to communicate and collaborate.

These include leadership acumen, emotional intelligence, teamwork, conflict management, sales and marketing, stress management, conflict resolution, negotiation skills, interpersonal skills, business development, time management, public speaking, decision-making, problem-solving techniques: creativity, and flexibility.

For instance, to excel in your career or business, you need to have the ability to communicate effectively with others. You might be a skilled chef, but if you cannot work well with a team, you will not be able to lead a restaurant team and achieve

INTRODUCTION

success. How we collaborate, communicate, and interact can affect our success in our personal or business life.

If you don't have these skills, it could decrease your success rate or cost you your current job. That is why those who have taken the time to learn the proper use of soft skills have been able to stand out and succeed, both in their careers and life.

This book will give you a complete understanding of soft skills and how they work. You'll also learn how to apply them appropriately to your situation, so you can get ahead of your competition and achieve everything you want.

1

COMMUNICATION SKILLS

"Communication is a skill that you can learn. It's like riding a bicycle or typing. If you're willing to work at it, you can rapidly improve the quality of every part of your life". Brian Tracy

FACTS & STATS

1. 86% of employees and executives cite the lack of effective communication and collaboration as the main causes for workplace failures.
2. Businesses using effective internal communication tools are 3.5 times more likely to have better results.
3. 97% of employees believe communication impacts their task efficacy on a daily basis.
4. 28% of employees cite poor communication as the reason for not being able to deliver work on time.
5. 65% of workers who received communication training at regular intervals report high-performance scores.

The word "communication" is derived from two words, "common" and "information." Communication is said to have taken place when the parties involved have common information. Communication is the skill that sustains information flow. Once there is a break in the communication process or chain, misunderstanding, confusion, and chaos are inevitable. Communication involves sharing thoughts, feelings, emotions, ideas, and information from one person to another with the possibility of receiving feedback. Communication is a two-way process; as such, you cannot claim to have communicated your idea to someone without feedback, either in agreement or disagreement.

The major cause of misunderstanding when communicating is the illusion that communication had occurred when your message was probably not understood. As a fresh graduate, a lot is expected of you; one of those basic expectations is the ability to communicate concisely and clearly when you engage with people, especially graduate recruiters. The first parameter for judging your level of articulation is how articulate you are and how effectively you communicate. You need to understand that good communication is two-way. Therefore, you have to be able to speak well and also be able to listen well.

Communication is not just what you say. It is also how you present yourself and how you say what you want to say. It also involves being able to phrase the right questions and developing your question-asking skills. A fresh graduate appearing before employers should know how to answer questions correctly. Avoid mincing words, so you don't confuse yourself and those listening. Learning not to say too much is also part of good communication, especially during interviews.

Excellent communication skills are the foundation of many other employable skills, including leadership and management, teamwork, relationship-building, and influencing skills. In developing good communication skills, you must become used to communicating with different audiences and changing your communication style when appropriate to suit your audience. There are different ways your communication skills will be accessed. It could be through verbal (that is what you say) or non-verbal communication (that is, written, body language, signs, symbols, postures, and gestures). As much as what you say is important, your non-verbal communication skills must be equally enhanced. Each time you appear before people to speak, no matter how tense you are, put up a warm smile and a confident posture that shows you know what you want to say.

Furthermore, learning how to communicate expressly through writing is also an important communication skill. Know how to share your thoughts precisely in writing, so you do not misinform your readers. As much as possible, avoid ambiguous words. Know the words that suit your audience or the person you are communicating with. Also, know that communication is more about listening and responding to others than talking and always wanting to be heard. Learn to concentrate on what others say, show you are listening through verbal or visual signs (nodding and giving a corresponding gesture), and build on what has been said. That goes to show that you are fully involved in the communication process. Avoid unnecessary digression. Ensure you stay on the subject of discourse by engaging in active listening.

Fresh graduates with strong communication skills will be able to settle disputes that may arise in their workplace. They will know the best approach to dealing with people and problem-solving. Good communicators are valuable assets to employers as they can take up vital managerial and leadership roles. Any graduate who is a skilled communicator can bridge the gap between the organization and the outside world or investors. This is because they will be excellent at negotiating change and persuading investors to take certain actions to benefit the organization.

Communication is an essential aspect of our everyday life, and as such, you must deliberately brace up your skills in communicating with people. This is not just to be employable but also to establish good relationships and enjoy peaceful co-existence with people. So, if you must be able to interact and build your communication skills effectively, do the following;

- **Constantly engage in conversations**

    The more you shy away from conversations; the poorer your communication skill becomes r. Learn to actively engage in meaningful conversations where you can develop your communication prowess. It could be a debate, speaking competition, or panel session. Create avenues to speak and engage people.

- **Engage in active listening to others**

   You communicate better when you are more concerned about what is being said than what you have to say. Communication is a two-way dialogue; you have a part to play by listening to the other person to understand their needs and opinions. Active listening will help you properly process the other person's thoughts to know how best to answer.

- **Reading**

   When you read, you widen your horizon and perspective about life. Read books, articles, and materials on how to improve your communication skills better and learn to practice what you've read.

- **Volunteering to do teamwork**

   Here is another platform where your communication skills can be enhanced. Volunteering to work with others involves communication. It will help you know how to deal with different people as you work together.

- **Participating in social functions**

   Social gatherings and activities like anchoring or co-hosting events will help you build your communication skills. You will do yourself and your employer a lot of good when you are an excellent communicator.

Action Point

Communication is key to opening many doors, one of which is employment. Graduates who have mastered the act of communicating will outshine their competitors.

2

INTERPERSONAL SKILLS

"Interpersonal skills are your windows to success. The way people perceive you depends on how you communicate with them. Working on this skill is the key to changing your life"- Rocky Saggo

FACT AND STATS

1. According to Mckinsey, 30 to 40% of future jobs will depend on interpersonal and socio-emotional skills.

2. Four trends are transforming your workplace. They are interpersonal skills (91%), work flexibility (72%), anti-harassment (71%), and pay transparency (53%)

3. 42% have voluntarily left a position because of a harsh and stressful working environment.

4. Job-related pressure, lack of managerial support, and workplace violence/bullying were among the leading catalysts for occupational stress.

5. 82% of employees show more commitment to work when management expresses genuine empathy.

Your interpersonal skill is an extension of your communication skill. You cannot build good interpersonal skills without first developing your communication skill. Good thing we've talked about communication skills earlier. Interpersonal skills are traits you rely on when interacting and communicating with others. These skills involve the ability to communicate and build relationships with others.

Interpersonal skills are often called people skills. Like I said earlier, you cannot avoid interacting with people no matter how hard you try. That is why you must develop your interpersonal skills to communicate well. Interpersonal skills are very important skill sets that fresh graduates should intentionally develop as they tend to incorporate both innate personality traits and how well they handle certain social situations. Employers are constantly looking for employees who can work well with others. Graduates with interpersonal skills will do very well at interview sessions, which can positively impact their career advancement.

Interpersonal skills enhance the face-to-face exchange of thoughts, ideas, feelings, and emotions between people. For fresh graduates desiring to enter the corporate world, building strong interpersonal skills will become an asset that can help you navigate complexity, change, and day-to-day tasks in your work environment. It will also help you adapt to the changing work environment and relate better with your colleagues.

Interpersonal skills will give you a better understanding of people and their different responses to situations and improve your ability to adjust your approaches to work together efficiently with people. Employers value interpersonal skills because they contribute to positive work environments and help maintain an efficient workflow. Graduates with technical (hard) and interpersonal skills are easily transferrable across industries and positions as they can easily adapt to changes and work with anyone.

Some of the interpersonal skills you can build to become employable and successful in your career development include;

    i. **Active listening**

        Listening is different from hearing. You can be hearing someone speaking but not listening. Listening involves paying rapt attention to a person by intentionally taking your mind off every form of distraction. Active listening has to do with your ability to listen to others to gather information and engage with the speaker. Active listening is an interpersonal skill that will help you communicate with people, as listening is a major part of communication. When you listen, you'll be able to identify the needs of others and know how well to relate with them.

ii. **Dependability**

This is another very vital interpersonal skill you can develop. Employers will make no mistake hiring someone who is not reliable and undependable. People should be able to rely on you in any given situation, especially as a fresh graduate trying to build a career for yourself.

iii. **Responsibility**

You must be able to take responsibility for your actions and the things under your control, especially in a work environment. Managers will not hire a careless fellow; they are looking for accountable people. This is one skill most young people lack. They tend not to be interested in the advancement of their organization and are just focused on the salary they hope to earn.

iv. **Empathy**

Employers may hire an empathetic or compassionate graduate to create a positive and high-functioning workplace. Understanding the needs and feelings of others will help you interact closely with customers and colleagues. This involves carefully studying people's moods before asking them for a favor to avoid getting a rash and annoying response.

v. **Leadership**

This is a very important interpersonal skill and will be discussed in subsequent pages. You cannot effectively lead people without first connecting with them. Interpersonal skills are essential for leaders; otherwise, winning and influencing people will be difficult.

vi. **Team working**

Working together as a team is extremely valuable in every organization. Those who are good team players are often given important tasks in the workplace and may be seen as good candidates for promotion.

vii. **Flexibility**

Adapting to changes in your workplace is a vital interpersonal skill to develop, as change is always constant. As a fresh graduate, be prepared to work anywhere at the entry-level. You may be required to work as a receptionist today and probably a marketer the next day. Your ability to switch roles and positions will keep you in an organization for a low time, as you will be valued for your flexibility.

viii. **Patience**

Your ability to be patient will be tested in diverse ways, especially when dealing with people and during prolonged interview sessions. You must learn to tolerate people and accommodate their excesses to maintain a peaceful work environment. Patience is a vital virtue you can build, and it will go a long way to open several doors for you in the future. Patience will teach you how to control your emotions when expressing anger and help you see the need for delayed gratification. Patience is key to enjoying successful deals with people.

Amongst the many criteria that will qualify you for that dream job, building your interpersonal skills is a top criterion for qualification. Therefore, now is the right time to start working on these skills by attending workshops, online classes, and seminars on personal development. Seek out opportunities to build relationships, and be thoughtful about ways your interactions with people could improve. Please do not give a lighthearted approach and an indifferent attitude about your interactions with others; take corrections when people bring them to your notice, observe other people's positive interpersonal skills and apply them.

You may also have to seek mentorship from trusted people you admire and respect. When you have someone you are accountable to, it helps you keep your actions in check. How people perceive you is very important, and one way to give people a good impression of you is by working on your interpersonal skills.

Action Point

Building interpersonal skills are essential for career advancement because as you climb up your career ladder, you'll meet different people. There's a need for effective interpersonal communication to sustain relationships and corporations.

3

NETWORKING/ SOCIALISING SKILLS

"Your network cannot be bought, borrowed, or downloaded like an app. You must create it through consistent action over time"- John Corcoran.

FACT AND STATS

1. 85% of professionals say that traditional networking both online and offline are essential for long-term business and career success.
2. 38% of professionals have difficulties staying in contact with their network, even though they realize it's important.
3. LinkedIn's research also confirms that most jobs are found through personal connections – 70% of them, to be precise!
4. Networking at business conferences, investment summits, trade shows and trade fairs can get you up to 25% of your new customers.
5. It may seem like business cards are a thing of the past. However, 68% of small business owners still find them impactful!

Building healthy relationships and network is an essential habit that must be learned. It is not just about making new friends and socializing but intentionally establishing certain meaningful contacts that could be relevant to your career pursuit. Networking is not about getting to know anyone who crosses your path in life but deliberately looking for ways to get into some influence cycles that will be valuable to your goals.

Many businesses and partnerships you see today were built on relationships and networking. As a fresh graduate beginning your career, you should make a conscious effort to get to know people, especially those you admire and would love to be in their cycle. Your goal for networking shouldn't be all about what you hope to get from your prospective networks but first about what you have to offer. Unfortunately, this is where most young people miss it. They tend to get into bad relationships for some wrong motives. If you are not a person of value, don't expect to attract people of value. Networking is hard work. If you are not networking, you are not working.

Now you've got the degree, concluded your national youth service, and sent a few CVs out, what next? This is the perfect time to start building meaningful networks. This is when you start career networking, it will help position you for career success. Networking is an effective way to kick-start your career as a fresh graduate. Fresh graduates often have no idea where to find the job they want. This is where networking comes to play. As the old saying goes, it isn't always about what you know but who you know.

For this reason and more, networking and cultivating productive relationships for employment and business purposes is a crucial factor for career success. This world as we see it today is a product of networking. It is an important and really common practice for working professionals. This is just the right time to start building solid relationships to open you up to a wide range of career opportunities, especially now that you're a fresh graduate.

Certain heights in your career may not be attained except through the people in your network. For your network is your net worth. Research shows that 70% to 80% of jobs are not advertised, meaning that if you want to know the vast majority of jobs out there you will need to find out such information from people in your network or social cycle. Hence, it is expedient that you start building such networks early in your career to better position you to hear about the unadvertised jobs.

You will need to be proactive and intentional about building your network and staying in touch with them once the relationship has been established. You may even need to deliberately attend certain social gatherings and functions to meet these people so you can constantly maintain close contact with them. It could be a tasking thing, but trust me, it is doable and will pay off well now or in the long run. It is worth it to dedicate at least an hour every day to building and growing your network. When you grow your network, your net worth increases. Someone once said, if you want to be rich, walk with nine rich persons, you'll certainly be the tenth. If you consciously work at it, this could be your reality, not just a cliché.

There are several ways you can improve your networking and socializing skills, let's look at a few of them.

- **Always be prepared for networking.**

One key way to kick start your networking goal is to be prepared always for networking. Networking could happen anywhere, it doesn't always have to be a professional conference or business seminar. *"You always have to be prepared for potential opportunities when they come"* says, Yissel Cirion, Career Services Acting Associate Director.

Do not let a lifetime opportunity pass you by because you failed to prepare. You should always learn to carry your CV, especially the soft copy on your phone, because you never can tell where you would need to drop it. As Joel Delgado puts it in his Dec 12, 2014 post *"Because of this, start thinking about crafting your elevator pitch, the thirty-second speech that sums up who you are, what you do, and what type of job you're hoping to have, you never know when you might need to make a case for yourself"*. Preparation is known to be a proven key to success. You cannot afford to be caught off guard. You also can't tell the class of people you'll meet at certain occasions and places, so it is just wise you prepare to network at all times.

- **Be conscious of your image and reputation.**

As fresh graduates being conscious of your image and reputation is another way of building your network. Be intentional about adding value to your life. You'll attract what you are. You need to start by having and building confidence in yourself that you can add value to the persons you meet. Therefore, you need to build for yourself an acceptable image and reputation. Be ready to provide value to the people you come in contact with. When you've thought about the class of people you want to be in their network, think of what value you have to offer them. Don't approach a prospective network without having any value to share. Be conscious of the kind of activities you involve yourself in especially on social media because these things go a long way to show the kind of person you are and what matters to you. Employers also go that far as to check your profile on social platforms to know who you are before they invite you for interviews. As a starter, ensure you build a good reputation for yourself.

- **Treat networking as an investment**

You must know that networking is an investment in yourself and in your future take it seriously. What you give to it is what you get. Make it a point of duty to establish valuable contacts. Intentionally put yourself out there, learn to sell yourself, and invest time in other people, from professionals in your fields, to professionals in other fields. Do not limit your network, create a diverse network as it will open you up to diverse people, diverse opportunities, diverse industries, and places.

- **Have a goal for networking**

A goal helps you measure the progress of your life and career. Have a goal for every network you establish and see that you work hard to achieve it. Is your goal to get mentored, gain employment or establish a relationship? You need to be specific about your networking goals. More so, set realistic goals you can achieve by being in that network. This will help you know what you want for every network you build so you do not get into the wrong cycles. You may also need to do regular appraisals and assessments of your network. Evaluate yourself to know if these networks have been profitable. If otherwise, think through where you must have possibly missed it or pull out where necessary.

Graduate recruiters seek to employ graduates with good networking and socializing skills as they will be good intermediaries between their companies and other local and international companies. To rise above the odds of getting hired quickly, your networking skills must be top-notch. Intentionally work at developing it.

Action Point

Have a clear picture of where you are going and consciously build networks early in life to help you achieve your career goals.

4

ORGANISATIONAL SKILLS

"Organization isn't about perfection, it's about efficiency, reducing stress and clutter, saving time and money, and improving your overall quality of life"- Christina Scalise.

FACTS AND STATS

1. 27% said they feel disorganized at work, and of those, 91 percent said they would be more effective and efficient if their workspace was better organized.

2. According to MayoClinic.com, there is a distinct connection between organizational skills and the individual's mental and physical health.

3. According to Forbes ASAP, the typical executive today wastes 150 hours a year, almost one month, searching for lost information.

4. 80% of the clutter in home and offices is a result of disorganization, not lack of space. However, using the correct organizational tools can improve productivity by 38%.

5. People who multi-task decrease their productivity by 20-40% are less efficient than those who focus on one project at a time.

Believe it or not, one of the most valuable skills employers look for in candidates when hiring is organization. No employer wants to employ a fresh graduate that will make a mess of his work environment rather, one that can ensure things are in the right order. Organizational skills are some of the most important and transferrable job skills fresh graduates must acquire. These skills encompass a set of capabilities that help a person plan, prioritize, and achieve his or her goals, which can save a company time and money.

Organizational skills are those related to creating structure and order, boosting productivity, and prioritizing tasks that must be completed immediately versus those that can be postponed, delegated to another person, or eliminated. Being organized as a person help you know what task needs to be done urgently, those to be delayed, delegated or eliminated.

Managers look for employees who can keep their work and desk organized and adjust quickly to a company's organizational structure. Adaptability is a strong prerequisite for developing organizational skills. No business can succeed to any degree without being properly organized. This is why graduates seeking employment should possess this skill. Being organized will help you maintain a healthy work-life balance. You will know how best to combine your job and other vital aspects of your life for maximal output and productivity.

Here, are some ways you can build a good organizational skill:

- **Self -Discipline**

The number one key to being organized is self-discipline. Developing organizational skills for securing your desired job begins with how self-disciplined you are. You must learn to discipline yourself and ensure that everything is in its place and there is a place for everything. Do you get irritated when things are scattered? How comfortable are you when your workspace is untidy with files littered everywhere? You cannot live an organized life when you are not disciplined. Being disciplined helps you know what to do and the right time to do it. It helps you better manage your time by following your schedule dutifully. A disciplined employee will know that work hours are not for cheap chatting with colleagues. He/she will know that pressing phones and Internet surfing during working hours is unacceptable. A self-disciplined person doesn't wait to receive instructions on what to do but knows what's to be done. If you must develop good organizational skills to effectively discharge your job be disciplined. In disciplining yourself you can cultivate the habit of writing a to-do list. It will better improve your organizational skills. Ensuring that you follow your to-do list no matter what comes up shows how disciplined you are.

- **Planning**

Planning and scheduling are the most important ways to build an effective organizational skill. Planning is key if you must be organized. A plan might be as simple as deciding which end of the hall to clean first, or it could be to chart corporate strategy for the next ten years. Whichever the case, planning is necessary for organizational development. An Organization is not just having a tidy desk, and maintaining a clean appearance, it also involves maintaining order, staying on track with deadlines, and being prepared at all times with systematic planning and scheduling. Planning saves time. When things are not in their appropriate place, you waste a lot of time trying to locate them when you need them. When you save time, you become efficient at work and create time for unplanned activities. The overall goal of being organized is to save time. No manager will employ a time waster. You will become a valuable employee if you can save time and money for your organization. Being a successful organizer has a lot to do with the ability to plan. The more time you have to plan something, the more successful you will be. Planning allows you to accommodate unexpected projects that might arise between your schedules.

- **Prioritizing**

In developing organizational skills, you need to learn to prioritize. Prioritizing helps you determine the most important tasks and which can wait. If you know how to prioritize you'll be able to break up your work into smaller pieces. Then you can focus on each task, one at a time, starting with the most important. Developing organizational skills through prioritizing lowers stress and frustration levels. You can easily get stressed out and frustrated when you have so much to do with little or no time especially when deadlines are involved. Prioritizing will help you maneuver your way through achieving your set goals.

Developing organizational skills especially as a starter keeps you in control of your workplace and space. Once you are in control and in charge, your ability to be focused is enhanced. People who lack an organized leader will easily get into trouble, chaos, and mishaps. If you cannot take charge of your work environment and responsibilities laid on you, you may be considered unfit for the job and easily replaced. Above all, developing organizational skills for your job will help you feel balanced and composed. Maintaining a balanced work-life is quite a difficult task, but being organized becomes much easier as you can give the right time to the right activities at the right time. Operating with a balanced mind and environment will increase your productivity.

A well-developed organizational skill will help you meet deadlines in your organization. Deadlines are a very important aspect of every workflow. Once you miss deadlines once or more it shows how disorganized you are. Deadlines help you channel the right energy to a given task to ensure it is met. You can only be effective at meeting deadlines if you are an organized employee. An employee who is not well organized will rather choose to make excuses for not meeting important deadlines.

Once you've developed this skill, you can emphasize it in job applications, resumes, cover letters, and interviews. Employees however may not be able to know you have this skill except you demonstrate it. You can do this by showing up early enough for interviews. This is the first and most important impression you give about yourself that shows you are organized. Another way you show you are organized is by ensuring you come with all the required documents needed to access your qualification for the job. Also, behaving in an orderly manner during interviews does not only show you are well mannered but also organized.

Apart from emphasizing this skill on your application or cv, you may also need to explain scenarios where you utilized your organizational skills in solving a problem and what the outcomes were. It's always not a good thing to work under pressure. You may not be able to get the desired results but when you can use this skill well, you can plan to achieve your goals. Showing that you have the skills a company is seeking will help you get hired and promoted.

Action Point

The productivity and success you achieve in pursuing your career is directly proportional to how well you use your organizational skills. How organized are you?

5

GOAL SETTING SKILLS

"The trouble with not having a goal is that you can spend your life running up and down the field of life and never score" – Bill Copeland

FACTS AND STATS

1. Only 3% of people have written goals and plans, and they earn 10 times more than people who have no goals at all.
2. Setting (S.M.A.R.T) **S**pecific, **M**easurable, **A**chievable, **R**elevant and Time Bound goals increases the chances of success by 62%.
3. 70% of people who set written goals are more likely to achieve them compared to those who do not write them down.
4. People who set personal and professional goals achieve more in less time than those who do not set goals.
5. The act of writing down and regularly reviewing goals increases the likelihood of achieving them by up to 95%.

Goal setting is a critical skill for anyone, especially fresh graduates who are just starting their careers. It involves defining what you want to achieve, creating a plan to reach those goals, and then taking action to make it happen.

Developing goal setting is a crucial step towards success and personal growth. The process of goal setting must follow some basic principles such as setting specific, measurable, and achievable targets, and establishing a plan to reach these targets. This chapter will discuss the key steps to developing effective goal setting.

Step 1: Determine Your Goals

The first step in developing goal setting is to determine what you want to achieve. Consider what is important to you and what you value. This can include career goals, financial goals, personal development goals, or any other area that you wish to focus on.

It is essential to set both short-term and long-term goals. Short-term goals provide immediate satisfaction and help build momentum towards achieving your long-term goals. Long-term goals provide a sense of direction and provide a clear picture of what you want to achieve in the future.

Step 2: Write down goals

Writing down your goals refers to the process of physically writing and documenting what you want to achieve in life and career. It is magical!

It does not only give you that sense of urgency but also helps to focus your attention and provides short-term motivation and excitement. Written goals compel you to select specific, measurable goals that are important to you in both the long and short term.

By making your goals tangible, you significantly increase your chances of successfully realizing them.

Step 3: Make Your Goals Specific and Measurable

Once you have determined what you want to achieve, it is essential to make your goals specific and measurable. This means that you need to be clear about what you want to achieve and how you will measure your progress. For example, instead of setting a general goal of "getting in shape," a specific and measurable goal would be "losing 10 pounds in the next six months" or I will additional $ 25,000 in the next 12 months.

Step 4: Make Your Goals Achievable

It is important to set achievable goals. This means setting targets that are realistic and achievable within the given time frame. It is essential to consider the resources you have available and to be realistic about what you can accomplish. Achievable goals should stretch you, but not so difficult that they become disheartening. For example, setting a goal of losing 10 pounds in one week may not achievable and will only lead to frustration and disappointment.

Step 5: Establish a Plan of Action

Once you have determined your specific and achievable goals, it is important to establish a plan of action. This includes breaking down your goals into smaller, more manageable steps and determining what actions you need to take to reach your goals.

Step 6: Set a Time Frame

Setting a time frame for achieving your goals is essential. This helps to create a sense of urgency and keeps you focused on what you need to do to reach your goals. It is important to set a realistic time frame and to regularly review your progress to ensure that you are on track. Napoleon Hill, The author of "Think and Grow Rich" said "A goal is a dream with a deadline".

Step 7: Monitor Your Progress

Monitoring your progress is an important part of the goal setting process. It allows you to track your progress and to make adjustments as needed. Regular progress tracking helps to keep you motivated and ensures that you are making progress towards achieving your goals.

Step 8: Celebrate Your Achievements

It is essential to celebrate your achievements along the way. Celebrating your progress helps to reinforce positive behavior and reinforces your commitment to your goals. It is also a great way to acknowledge the hard work that you have put into reaching your goals.

Why People Don't Set Goals

By understanding these common barriers to goal setting, fresh graduates can take steps to overcome them and start setting goals that aligns with desires and aspirations.

- **Lack of clarity:** Many people struggle with identifying their goals, either because they don't know what they want or because they are overwhelmed by the options available to them.

- **Fear of failure:** Setting goals can be intimidating, especially if you fear that you won't be able to achieve them. This fear can keep people from setting goals altogether.

- **Lack of motivation:** Without a clear sense of purpose or direction, it can be difficult to find the motivation to set goals and work towards achieving them.

- **Poor time management:** People who struggle with time management may find it difficult to set goals, as they may not have the time or energy to focus on them.

- Procrastination: Procrastination is a common reason why people don't set goals, as they may put off setting goals because they are too busy or simply don't feel like it.

- Lack of confidence: Low self-esteem or a lack of confidence can make it difficult to set and pursue goals, as people may feel that they are not capable of achieving what they set out to do.

- Resistance to change: People may resist setting goals because they are comfortable with their current situation and are afraid of change.

- Priorities: People may not set goals because they have other priorities in their life that take precedence, such as family or work obligations.

- Disorganization: People who struggle with disorganization may find it difficult to set and follow through on goals, as they may not have a clear plan or system in place.

- Poor planning skills: People who lack effective planning skills may struggle to set and achieve their goals, as they may not have a clear roadmap for how to get there.

Seven Key Areas You Must Consider When Setting Goals:

1. Career/Professional Development goals refer to aspirations and targets related to one's work and career. These may include seeking promotions, acquiring new skills and knowledge, finding better job opportunities, increasing job satisfaction, and achieving work-life balance. Setting career goals can help an individual stay focused, motivated, and track their progress towards their desired professional growth and success.

2. Financial goals refer to targets related to managing one's financial resources effectively. These may include saving for emergencies, paying off debt, planning for retirement, building wealth, and creating a budget. Setting financial goals can help an individual make informed decisions about their money, prioritize their spending, and ensure long-term financial stability and security. Achieving financial goals often requires planning, discipline, and consistent effort over time.

3. Health and Physical Wellness goals refer to aspirations related to maintaining good health and fitness. These may include eating a balanced diet, exercising regularly, getting enough sleep, managing stress, and avoiding harmful habits such as smoking and excessive alcohol consumption. Setting health goals can help an individual improve their physical and mental well-being, boost their energy levels, and prevent chronic health conditions. Achieving health and physical wellness goals often requires making lifestyle changes, being proactive about one's health, and seeking support when needed.

4. Relationships and Social Life goals refer to aspirations related to personal relationships and social interactions. These may include maintaining strong relationships with friends and family, meeting new people, forming new romantic relationships, developing communication skills, and improving conflict resolution abilities. Setting goals for

relationships and social life can help an individual build meaningful connections, expand their social network, and enhance their overall sense of community and belonging. Achieving these goals often requires making time for others, being open and honest in communication, and working on personal growth and self-improvement.

5. Spiritual goals refer to aspirations related to one's spiritual or religious beliefs, values, and practices. These may include finding inner peace, developing a deeper connection with a higher power, becoming more compassionate and charitable, and engaging in spiritual practices such as meditation, prayer, or service. Setting spiritual goals can help an individual strengthen their beliefs, improve their well-being, and live a more fulfilling life. Achieving spiritual goals often requires committing to personal growth, seeking guidance and support, and being open to new experiences and perspectives.

6. Community Involvement goals refer to aspirations related to contributing to one's community and making a positive impact in the world. These may include volunteering, participating in community events, supporting local businesses, and advocating for important causes. Setting community involvement goals can help an individual feel more connected to their community, develop new skills and relationships, and make a difference in the lives of others. Achieving these goals often requires being proactive, seeking opportunities to give back, and being open to new experiences and perspectives.

7. Personal Growth and Learning goals refer to aspirations related to self-improvement and personal development. These may include developing new skills, learning new subjects, overcoming personal challenges, setting and achieving personal milestones, and becoming a better version of oneself.

Setting personal growth and learning goals can help an individual enhance their abilities, increase their self-awareness, and live a more fulfilling life. Achieving these goals often requires setting clear targets, seeking new experiences and opportunities, and being open to feedback and self-reflection.

Action Point

You must set goals that are almost impossible to achieve. If you set goals that are easily attainable without much thought or effort, you will be limited to something that is below your true talent and potential.

6

PROBLEM SOLVING SKILLS

"Every problem has a solution. You just have to be creative enough to find it"- Travis Kalanick.

FACTS AND STATS

1. Every situation has a solution - they may not be the desired outcome, but no matter what, there are still ways to solve the problem.

2. Only 45% of employees come up with creative and effective solutions to identified problems, recognizing what needs to be done before taking action.

3. 20% of your time will be spent on 80% of your solution. 80% of your time will be spent on the last 20% of the solution. The next key question to ask is, can you get by with an 80% solution?

4. It's not enough to solve our problems with the same level of thinking that created them. 60% tend to use old strategies for new challenges.

5. There are a lot of ways to solve any problem and your understanding of the "actual problem" increases the chances of solution by 70%.

Problem-solving skills are one of the most basic skills you weren't taught in school. This accounts for why a lot of youths are unemployed. They've refused to open up their minds to opportunities hidden in solving a problem. It's unfortunate today to see young people debating and arguing about the country's prevailing problems, but no one is looking for possible solutions. They think if they continually shy away from the problem it will eventually go away so rather than creatively thinking of a way out, they resolve to ignore the problem. A problem ignored is never a problem solved, it eventually gives room for more problems.

The Collins English dictionary defines problem-solving as finding solutions to problems, especially using a scientific or analytical approach. It is a vital everyday skill fresh graduates must have in their personal and professional lives. Problem-solving involves critical and analytical thinking which is why many young people run from it as they consider it cumbersome and brain-tasking. There is a lot of competition in the corporate world, one way to stand out is by developing the mindset of a problem solver. Problem solvers are very optimist people. They always look for a way out and the truth is there is always a way out. It will only cost you a bit of hard work and creativity in figuring out a solution.

Developing problem-solving skills is necessary for fresh graduates because employers like to see good problem-solving skills as it tells them you have other competencies such as:

- **Logic**

Problem-solving involves a lot of logical reasoning and thinking to deduce a possible solution. This requires you to research the cause of the problem properly, gathering relevant facts on how it can be solved. Graduates desiring to build a career in architecture, engineering, quantity surveying, and other related fields will require a lot of logical thinking.

- **Creativity**

The process of problem-solving will demand creative thinking as well. There are creative approaches to solving a problem so that it doesn't cause further problems. This can be done by seeing the problem as an opportunity to create a change or chart a new course. Creativity should be employed in problem-solving if you want to remain valuable in your field.

- **Resilience**

It takes a resilient mind to figure out a solution. People are always quick to give up on the problem than painstakingly looking for a solution or a possible way out. One must have a die-hard attitude and be dogged to get results in solving a problem.

- **Imagination**

Sometimes you need to engage your mind in imaginary thinking to get solutions. It begins with imagining how feasible the proposed solution will be, what the outcome will be, whether it will cause more problems. What is important is that you need to engage your mind to birth a solution.

- **Determination**

There is always a solution to every problem. The question is how determined are you? Determination is what you need to find a solution. It may take a long time, even longer than expected, so do not get discouraged. A fresh graduate determined to solve problems in his/her organization could be considered worthy of promotion when the need arises.

Problem-solving skill is a skill that is accessed during job interviews. Therefore, you must determine to make it a part of your qualifications. Those with excellent problem-solving skills are valuable and trusted assets in any team. They are the people who think of new ideas, better ways of doing things. They make it easier for people to understand things and save customers time and money.

Problem solvers are proactive thinkers who like to get things done. Graduates who have mastered this skill progress more quickly than their contemporaries, boosting their career opportunities. One thing you should understand is that problem solving is a process. It is a mental process involving discovering and analyzing until a solution is proposed. Every organization is bound to encounter a problem at one time or the other. You could earn a promotion or salary increase if you are found relevant in solving your organization's problems.

The ultimate goal of problem-solving is to overcome obstacles and find a solution that best resolves the issue. When you are found worthy, your boss may want to trust you with more responsibilities or consider you for a managerial role later. Do not ever think you are too small to proffer a solution in your workplace. While you will not likely be asked to find a solution to a major issue, handling even the smallest of problems will go a long way to demonstrate to your boss how well you can deal with larger ones. So, start by solving the little issues you face every day. Knowing how to solve problems is therefore of paramount importance in every organization. You can develop this skill if you put your mind to it. You can easily build your problem-solving ability through gaming, either online or with classic board games. As funny or stupid as this may sound, it does works. Putting yourself in a situation even a fictional one, where you have to think creatively will help you develop the same mindset in your everyday life. You can also apply these skills and behaviors to your professional life. Do not run away from problems. We all tend to want to hide instead of facing the problem and coming up with a solution. Rather choose to deal with it promptly before it escalates, instead of running away from it. Running from your problems does not make it automatically go away. Learn to welcome advice, listen to what people with experience say. It will save you a whole lot of trouble in solving a problem.

Lastly, stay out of problems. Do not live all your life solving problems you could have avoided. Demonstrating that you are a great problem solver is not always easy. Your ability to think on your feet, remain calm in stressful situations, and contributing to finding a solution is a possible way to do that. Problem-solving opens you up to new opportunities and possibly promotions. The more problems you solve, the better you develop this skill. Do not get comfortable and relax each time there is a problem to be solved in your workplace. Take it upon yourself to find a temporary or permanent solution to the problem. Problems ignored will always lead to more problems, ensure you find a solution.

Action Point

Behind every problem, there is an opportunity. Look beyond the problem, rather choose to see an opportunity that will better your life.

7

DECISION-MAKING SKILLS

"It is better to be approximately right than precisely wrong"- Warren Buffet.

FACTS AND STATS

1. A survey conducted by the Harvard Business Review, 72% of respondents said that decision-making is the most important leadership skill.

2. Researchers found that that the smaller a decision making group is, the more likely the group is to make the right choice

3. A study by the University of California found that people make an average of 70 decisions per day.

4. According to a survey by YouGov, 75% of people struggle with making decisions.

A study by neuroscientist Antonio Damasio found that decisions become almost impossible when they're only reduced to logic

Decision making is a core skill that every graduate must use at some stage in their career. The decision you choose to accommodate whatever situation you find yourself in can either take you up or pull you down. Decision-making is a very delicate aspect of one's life and must be treated with caution. Every business's success or failure relies on decisions made. At some point in your career as a graduate, you will be required to take certain critical decisions.

The quality of your decision will determine what your career will become in the coming years. That is why you must be careful in making any decision. You will need to prove that you are good at decision-making and to prove this, you will need to make the best possible choice in the shortest time possible, as well as being able to show reasons that support your decisions. It is a very tough state to be found. Sometimes as an employee, you will be forced to make complex decisions routinely as part of your job description, even under intense pressure. This is why it is necessary to build firm decision-making skills now that you still have the time to avoid losing your job due to poor decisions.

Every employer wants to be sure that the people they employ or recruit can take the initiative required and make good decisions in an important situation so you must ensure you work at developing this vital skill. Top managerial positions and promotions often come with making tough and complex decisions in difficult times that eventually turned out to be right for the company and business. To function in such a rank, you must learn to make decisions and ensure that your decisions are right for the company.

Decision-making is a fundamental aspect of the management role. Fresh graduates who aspire for such roles need to measure up to the responsibility that comes with it. Good decision-making is crucial in day-to-day business and must be handled expertly. Decision-making is a skill that employers value because it will be required in many situations across many business areas. From everyday tasks to more complex projects or unforeseen situations. Your ability to make effective decisions regardless of the scenarios makes you outsmart your contemporaries.

There are three ways in which you make decisions they are:

i. Intuition

This type of decision-making is handy when you have to make a quick decision or you have a considerable amount of experience that enables you to make a snap judgment of the situation. It is also called the sixth sense. When you decide intuitively, you can gather the information that other individuals may miss but which you got in on using your guts and instincts.

ii. Logic

This has to do with using logic to make choices. It uses evidence and facts to develop arguments and reasons to conclude before deciding. Your ability to use logical reasoning will be useful in certain types of employment such as in the legal sector or consulting.

iii. Cognitive bias

This type of error in thinking occurs when people are processing and interpreting information in the world around them. It is often a result of the attempt of the brain to simplify information processing.

Whichever way you choose to make your decision whether through intuition, logic, or cognitive bias, ensure it is the right thing to do to avoid causing problems for yourself and your organization. Carefully think through the process before deciding. To be effective in your decision-making process, have adequate information about the subject or issue you are to decide on. Take time to collect the necessary data even if you have a particularly short deadline. Also, do not overload yourself with too much information as it can prove detrimental to the decision-making process.

You can also learn to break up more complex decisions into easier-to-manage steps and effectively plan decision-making before settling on the decision made. Planning is an efficient tool for decision-making and anything else in life. In planning, you will be able to determine the likely outcomes of your decision and properly think through to better make a choice. It will afford you enough time to gather your facts, pieces of evidence, and data before arriving at a decision. Once a decision is made, it might be difficult to go back on it as it may prove your decision-making powers to be weak and people will begin to doubt your ability to make quality decisions. That is why you must carefully think through the process before reaching a judgment.

Many businesses have failed due to wrong decisions made, some went bankrupt and met with misfortunes due to bad choices. That is why thriving businesses have professionals set as a board of directors to be able to make sound decisions that will help the company achieve its vision. A company's vision that is why employers appreciate employees who can drive an organization from one point to another through quality decision-making.

A fresh graduate who can make sound judgments will be easily employed. But before you get there you must start by evaluating your everyday decisions and how they impact your life. You cannot be allowed to decide the affairs of an organization when you've not made a simple decision on who your friends will be. It starts with the everyday decisions you make to the more complex ones. Regularly assess the choices you've made and what the outcomes were so you can evaluate your decision-making ability. This will enable you to improve on areas where you've most likely made poor decisions and identify areas where your decision power is strong.

Furthermore, you will make poor decisions when your decisions are emotionally based and biased rather than factual especially in a work environment. When making a very critical decision for your organization it must not be based on your feelings or emotions, they could be wrong. Its best it's logical and based on available pieces of evidence. Once your decision is void of bias and emotions, people will begin to trust and respect your decision power. And when you say let us go this way and not that way, they won't be able to question you if your decisions have been proven right.

Fresh graduates should bear in mind that the success of their career is dependent on the decisions they make. The quality of your decisions today proves what your life will be like tomorrow. Your decision is your power, make sound use of it.

Action Point

You are a product of your decision, what you decide is what you become.

8

LEADERSHIP SKILLS

"A leader knows the way, goes the way, and shows the way"- John C. Maxwell.

FACTS AND STATS

1. 83% of companies' chief executive officers say developing leaders is fundamental. Yet less than 5% of companies have implemented leadership development across all levels.
2. 78% of business leaders actively and regularly focus on engaging with their employees.
3. 69% of employees say they would work harder if they felt their efforts were better recognized.
4. 33% of companies with strategic and consistent employee engagement are 22% more profitable.
5. 63% of Millennials believe their leadership skills are not being fully tapped and developed.

Research showed that leadership skills ranked high in the NACE (National Association of Colleges and Employers) report. Leadership skills are not just for those being interviewed for managerial jobs but are also important for all posts. It is a skill that employers consider in all candidates regardless of the position they have applied for. Employers are looking for fresh graduates who show the potential to be team leaders in the future. Leadership skills show that you are a self-starter and can handle decision-making well. This means you can motivate yourself and others well and make quality decisions for those you lead.

A leader knows the way and has what it takes to show others the way. Leadership is about responsibility and way beyond position. Leadership is having a burden for others, it is all about the people you intend to influence through your leadership style and skills. You do not necessarily have to be in a leadership position to possess this skill. You can lead people without occupying a position but being in a position will help you make certain changes and do things you ordinarily may not have the privilege to do.

Michael Hyatt's five marks of authentic leadership shows what you should look out for in every leader. Though some persons are born leaders, others were taught or trained to be leaders. Whichever category you fall under, these five leadership marks should be demonstrated in your leadership. They are:

- **Influence**

Leadership is a position of influence. You either influence people positively or negatively. Leaders are strong influencers, they influence others' actions, decisions, and lifestyles. Employers are interested in employees who can influence their colleagues, customers, and investors to take certain actions to improve the company's productivity. To be able to influence others, you must be a leader with strong character. Character is the bedrock of good leadership. It is what defines a leader. You influence people through your character. Developing a strong character will be a better influencer to people.

- **Impact**

Leadership is basically about impact. If you have nothing to show for your years of leadership, you have successfully failed as a leader. Leaders are result-oriented and look for ways to impact the lives of the people and the organization they lead. True leaders are known for the impact they create by being able to cause remarkable and positive change in their organization. In demonstrating your leadership skills, you must be prepared to create an impact through your actions. Employers should be able to recognize your impact and reward you accordingly. The more impact you make in your organization, the more relevant you become and the harder it is to dismiss you.

- **Insight**

Leaders are visionaries and very insightful. They have insight into the future they want to create. Graduates with superior ability to see into the future and prepare for what they want to achieve will stand a chance to get into leadership positions in their company.

- **Initiative**

Your ability to develop creative ideas and initiatives that will chart a new course for your company will increase your chances of getting picked for the job. Building your leadership skills requires good initiatives and plans for advancing your organization. Leadership skills involve being skilled to take initiatives and challenges. As a leader, you must be able to come up with initiatives that will better improve the workflow and also those that will help resolve challenges and conflicts that may arise in the course of working.

- **Integrity**

In this competitive world we are in today, leaders with integrity are highly valued. One of the hallmarks of a good leader is integrity. When people can hold you by your words. When they do not doubt your person and character, you can be considered for leadership positions sooner than expected. Employers desire to have leaders with integrity run their businesses, whether they are present or absent, they are at peace.

Developing strong leadership skills will help you attain certain positions and promotions in your career. Leadership skills if possessed will guide you within an organization. Taking the lead in your workplace will demand that you engage in certain tasks. Some of which are:

- **Possessing leadership skills in a work environment means the ability to motivate the team**

Every leader must first be self-motivated to motivate others despite the unpleasant situations of the workplace, a leader must be able to motivate the team to get the job done at the right time with the desired results. Employers are keen on employees who can motivate others. They assign special duties to them because they can always count on their deliverability.

- **Possessing leadership skills involves being able to delegate tasks**

Being a leader does not mean you must be the one to do all the activities. You must know what tasks to delegate and those you should do yourself to enjoy a smooth workflow. Also, knowing the right persons to delegate for certain jobs is very important as this can haunt your decision power and the organization's overall productivity.

- **Possessing leadership skills is demonstrated through examples**

You have to set an example for others through their work understanding. Leaders with work acumen develop their knowledge of all areas of the work operations to lead others. Leadership is more of what you do than what you say.

Developing good leadership skills is by examples. You must live exemplary lives, worthy of emulation. A leader who comes late for meetings and scolds his subordinate for coming a few minutes later is no different from the employee. Leadership by example means doing what you will appreciate when others do the same.

Fresh graduates must show potential to motivate teams and colleagues that may work for them. It's about assigning and delegating tasks well, setting deadlines, and leading by good examples. Though leadership ability is inherent, it can also be acquired by training, experience, and skill development.

Action Point

To build strong leadership skills, build strong character.

9

BUSINESS WRITING SKILLS

"You can have brilliant ideas, but if you can't get them across, your ideas won't get you anywhere. - Lee Iacocca.

FACTS AND STATS

1. According to a survey by Adecco Staffing, 59% of hiring managers believe that poor writing skills are a barrier to career advancement.
2. The average person reads about 300 words per minute, but can write at a pace of only about 40-60 words per minute.
3. A study by the National Survey of Student Engagement found that only 45% of college students report that they have frequently written papers longer than 5 pages.
4. In a survey by the National Association of Colleges and Employers, 94% of employers said they consider strong writing skills to be very important when hiring recent college graduates.
5. A survey by the Society for Human Resource Management found that 56% of companies provided writing training for their employees.

Business writing is an essential skill for fresh graduates who are looking to start their careers. Effective business writing is crucial to communicating ideas, persuading others, and making a good impression in the workplace. Whether you're writing emails, memos, reports, or presentations, it's important to understand the fundamentals of business writing.

When PayScale surveyed nearly 64,000 managers for its 2016 survey, 44% of them said recent college graduates lacked proficiency in writing. While programming and other tech-related skills are often listed as the most valuable skills a person can have writing is viewed as a more essential skill. Even people in non-writing roles need to be able to write. Fresh graduates should add a few more writing classes to their schedule if they want to prepare for full-time work. Many managers look at cover letters more to assess writing skills than to learn additional details about the candidate. In this chapter, we'll discuss the step-by-step guide to improving your business writing skills as a fresh graduate.

- **Step 1: Understanding the Audience**

Before you start writing, it's important to understand who your audience is. This includes their background, education, experience, and any other factors that might affect how they perceive your message. Understanding your audience will help you tailor your writing to their needs and interests.

- **Step 2: Clarity and Conciseness**

Clear and concise writing is crucial for effective communication in the workplace. You should aim to use simple language and avoid jargon or technical terms that your audience may not understand. It's also important to be concise and get to the point quickly. This means eliminating unnecessary words and phrases that don't add value to your message.

- **Step 3: Grammar and Punctuation**

Proper grammar and punctuation are essential for professional writing. Mistakes in grammar and punctuation can detract from your message and make you appear unprofessional. You should review your writing carefully and use grammar and spell check tools to ensure your writing is error-free.

- **Step 4: Tone and Style**

The tone and style of your writing can have a significant impact on how your message is received. Your tone should be appropriate for the audience and the situation. It's important to be professional but also personable and friendly. Your writing style should be consistent and easy to read, with a logical flow of ideas.

- **Step 5: Organization and Structure**

Organizing your writing in a logical structure is important for clarity and easy comprehension. You should use headings, subheadings, and bullet points to break up the text and make it more digestible for the reader. A clear structure will help the reader understand the main points of your message and follow your argument.

- **Step 6: Writing Emails**

Email is a common form of communication in the workplace. Writing effective emails is crucial for making a good impression and getting your message across. You should use a clear subject line, a professional greeting, and a concise message. It's also important to proofread your email before sending it and to avoid using all caps or excessive exclamation marks.

- **Step 7: Writing Memos and Reports**

Memos and reports are often used for more formal communication in the workplace. These types of documents require a more formal tone and structure. You should include an introduction, main points, and a conclusion, and use headings and bullet points to break up the text. It's important to be clear, concise, and organized in your writing.

- **Step 8: Writing Presentations**

Presentations are a common form of communication in the workplace. Effective presentations require careful planning and preparation. You should start by outlining your key points and creating a clear structure for your presentation. It's important to use visuals, such as charts or graphs, to illustrate your points and engage the audience. Your presentation should be clear, concise, and engaging.

- **Step 9: Practice Writing**

One of the best ways to improve your business writing skills is to practice writing regularly. You can start by writing emails or memos to colleagues or even drafting articles or blog posts for personal or professional purposes. The more you write, the better you will become at organizing your thoughts, conveying your message, and engaging your audience.

- **Step 10: Read Widely**

Reading widely can help you improve your business writing skills by exposing you to different writing styles and techniques. You can read business books, articles, reports, and blogs to see how other writers communicate effectively. Pay attention to their use of language, tone, and structure, and try to incorporate what you learn into your own writing. Reading broadens your perspectives. It enables you to know the right choice of words, writing skills, and techniques to employ when writing. Words are the lifeblood of great writers. If you want to be a wordsmith, read.

- **Step 11: Seek Feedback**

Getting feedback from others can help you improve your business writing skills by identifying areas for improvement. You can ask colleagues, supervisors, or even friends to review your writing and provide feedback on its clarity, organization, and style. You can also use online writing tools or resources to get feedback on your grammar and punctuation

- **Step 12: Revise and Edit**

Effective business writing requires careful revision and editing. After you've written your first draft, take the time to review it and make any necessary changes. This could involve reorganizing the structure, cutting unnecessary words or sentences, or adding more detail where needed. You should also proofread your writing carefully to ensure that there are no errors in grammar, spelling, or punctuation.

- **Step 13: Use Templates**

Using templates can be a great way to improve your business writing skills by providing you with a structured format to follow. Many email programs, word processors, and presentation software come with pre-designed templates that you can use to create professional-looking documents. You can also create your own templates for specific types of communication, such as memos or reports.

- **Step 14: Attend Workshops or Training**

If you feel like you need more help in improving your business writing skills, you can attend workshops or training sessions. Many companies offer in-house training on business writing, and there are also online courses and webinars that you can take. These can help you develop your skills and provide you with feedback from experts in the field.

- **Step 15: Some Practical Tips**

    <u>Tone and Style</u>

    Good example:

    Dear Mr. Smith, I hope this email finds you well. I'm writing to follow up on our meeting last week and to provide you with the information you requested.

    Bad example:

    Hey Smith, what's up? Just wanted to hit you up about our meeting last week. Here's the info you asked for.

    <u>Organization and Structure</u>

    Good example:

    Introduction: Background on the issue.

    Body: Main points and supporting evidence.

    Conclusion: Summary and next steps.

    Bad example:

    Rambling paragraphs that jump from one idea to another without a clear structure or organization.

    <u>Clear and Concise Language</u>

    Good example:

    Please send me the report by Friday.

Bad example:

It would be greatly appreciated if you could send me the report by the end of this week, as I will need it for a meeting on Monday.

Active Voice

Good example:

I will contact the client tomorrow to discuss the proposal.

Bad example:

The client will be contacted tomorrow to discuss the proposal.

Proofread Carefully

Good example:

Dear Ms. Lee,

Thank you for taking the time to meet with me yesterday. As per our conversation, I have attached a summary of the project for your review. Please let me know if you have any questions or concerns.

Bad example:

Dear Ms. Lee,

Thank you for meeting with me yesterday. As we discuss, I have attached a summery of the project for your reveiw. Please let me know if you have any questions or concerns.

Improving your business writing skills is an ongoing process that requires practice, feedback, and continuous learning. Whether you're writing emails, memos, reports, or presentations, it's important to understand your audience, be clear and concise, use proper grammar and punctuation, have an appropriate tone and style, use a logical structure, and tailor your writing to the situation. By following these steps, fresh graduates can improve their business writing skills and make a positive impact in the workplace. With practice and persistence, you can become a more effective and confident business writer.

Action Point

You must be intentional in honing your writing skills. According to "Seth Godin The reason business writing is horrible is that people are afraid. Afraid to say what they mean, because they might be criticized for it. Afraid to be misunderstood, to be accused of saying what they didn't mean, because they might be criticized for it."

10

NEGOTIATION SKILLS

"Let us never negotiate out of fear. But let us never fear to negotiate"- JOHN F. Kennedy.

FACTS AND STATS

1. Negotiation skills are important in both personal and professional settings.

2. According to a survey by the Harvard Negotiation Project, 92% of people believe they are good negotiators, but only 10% actually are.

3. A study by the International Management Association found that effective negotiation can increase a person's salary by up to 20%.

4. Negotiation skills can be improved through education, practice, and seeking feedback from others.

A survey by the Negotiation Institute found that the average person is involved in over 100 negotiations per year.

The whole concept of negotiating is intimidating to many people, and many people run away from negotiating for fear of losing their stand or giving in to their opponents. Negotiation is a discussion to settle disputes and reach agreements between two or more parties. Generally, a negotiation results in a compromise for the benefit of everyone involved.

Negotiation skills allow two or more parties to reach a compromise. Negotiation is a life skill in many areas. In life, we are constantly negotiating whether we realize it or not and it is one skill every graduate must develop to enable them to get better career opportunities. Negotiation shouldn't be a scary thing to do but rather should be seen as agreeing. The moment you see negotiation as simply reaching an agreement, it becomes interesting.

Negotiation skills involve certain abilities such as communication, persuasion, planning, strategizing, and corporation. Understanding these skills is the first step to becoming a stronger negotiator.

- **Communication**

You must effectively know how to communicate your deal by expressing yourself in a very engaging way. You must establish a clear communication flow to avoid misunderstandings that could prevent you from reaching a compromise. Communication as earlier discussed is a vital part of everyday living, without which social interaction is impaired. This also applies to negotiation. You must be able to express your terms of negotiations in simple and clear English or whatever form of language is employed. Employees will be required to do biddings and closing of deals for their company, and as such the communication flow must be sustained to reach a compromise.

- **Persuasion**

This is another vital key in negotiation. The ability to persuade others to take certain actions is crucial for successful negotiation. This will help you properly define why your proposed solution will benefit both parties. Persuasion cannot be done with mere words of mouth but with facts and proof. You must convince the other parties that you have a superior offer and give them reasons why they should give in to your offer. You can win and influence people when you pay attention to their concerns through listening. In doing so, you'll identify the best persuasive approach to employ in negotiation.

- **Planning and strategizing**

This is not just necessary for negotiation processes but also for deciding how the terms will be carried. Hence, you must plan your negotiation, consider all possible outcomes, and be prepared for them. Planning is yet considered another vital aspect of negotiation. You will be easily carried away and swept off your feet with ridiculous offers if you do not properly plan your negotiation. What planning helps you do is to offer you the opportunity to research the parties you are to negotiate with and other important facts your negotiation must be hanging on.

- **Corporation**

Negotiation involves much cooperation from both parties to arrive at a compromise. It may be difficult to reach an agreement where both parties are not cooperating. You must know how best to cooperate with the other party to avoid disagreement. Knowing there will be a need for compromise should encourage both parties to cooperate to achieve their negotiation goals.

As fresh graduates entering the corporate world, building firm negotiation skills cannot be overemphasized as it will be required in basically all you need to do not just for salary issues. Most negotiation outcomes will fall into two categories; win-win or win-lose. You must be sure of your desired outcome and adequately prepare for it. If you desire to win and not to lose, then be prepared to do all that is required to win.

To be able to successfully improve on your negotiation skills, you may need to take certain steps.

- **Identify the final goal of your negotiations**

The goal of every negotiation must be known. You must identify the goal of your negotiation by knowing what you want from an agreement and how much you're willing to compromise. Having this understanding will set you in an advantaged position when negotiating.

- **Learn to build rapport between the party or parties involved**

    Intentionally build a good rapport with the party or parties you are negotiating with by actively listening to understand their wants and needs. Before the negotiation starts, you can engage in petty talks to make the other person feel comfortable to continue the negotiation.

- **Be willing to compromise**

    Without compromise, it can be impossible to reach an agreement. The ultimate goal of every negotiation is to reach a compromise. This can be made possible when both parties see a need to. Otherwise, it becomes extremely difficult to do. Sometimes you will need to let go for the other person in anticipation of a greater future good. Compromising doesn't mean you lost but only means you are ready to reach an agreement peacefully.

- **Exercise confidence**

    You should learn to exercise confidence when negotiating especially when it has to do with salary negotiations. It can be challenging to ask for what you want. But to be successful at negotiating, you need to exercise high confidence and self-assurance. Do not be afraid to ask or state your terms during negotiations else you appear weak and unprepared for negotiating.

- **Practice often**

    One of the best ways to increase your comfort in negotiations is to practice often. You cannot get better at negotiating except you learn to do it as often as possible.

You can practice negotiations with friends and families regularly. This will better prepare you when bigger opportunities for negotiating comes.

Furthermore, always be prepared for every negotiation. Know what you want to gain, know where you are willing to compromise. Understand the terms you refuse to accept as well as all possible outcomes. It is also important to know when to walk away when the need arises and always have a timeline you must keep, regardless of the outcomes.

The workplace is ever-changing, but negotiation remains constant. This skill can help you develop your career, secure a higher salary and meet crucial business needs. Continuous practice is key to improving your negotiation ability. So, when next you are on this table, eradicate every form of fear and do your bidding boldly. It is either a win-win or a win-lose. Decide your outcomes, the choice is yours.

Action Point

Negotiation takes you from one level to another in advancing your career. The better you get at it, the higher you go.

11

SELLING SKILLS

"Approach each customer with the idea of helping him or her solve a problem or achieve a goal, not selling a product or service"- Brian Tracy.

FACTS AND STATS

1. According to a study by the National Sales Executive Association, the average salesperson spends only 34% of their time actually selling.
2. A survey by the Sales Management Association found that effective selling skills can increase a salesperson's productivity by up to 20%.
3. A study by the National Retail Federation found that the average sales conversion rate for retail businesses is 2-3%.
4. A survey by the International Marketing Association found that relationship building is a key component of successful selling.
5. The Bureau of Labor Statistics projects that employment of sales representatives will grow 3% from 2019 to 2029, which is about as fast as the average for all occupations.

Sales are not about selling anymore even if that is important. It is more about building trust and solving a problem. It is about conversing with people and helping them improve their company or lives. When you look at it from this perspective, selling becomes a very admirable task. Money shouldn't be the only outcome of your sales. It must transcend beyond that into building trust and integrity. While so many people are busy focusing on selling their goods or services, others are busy building trust and integrity through one sale. These sets of people understand that once trust and integrity are built, selling becomes a work-over as you will get referrals from far and near from just one sale. Getting people to refer you to render a service or deliver a product is a huge platform for selling which, unfortunately, so many people neglect.

Developing a career in sales can be key to long-term stability and prosperity. You can make your way up to sales executive jobs from that first job. You can't achieve that if you focus only on the figures you'll make from each sale. If you do so, you probably will not get to the upper echelon of your desired career.

Selling skills are specific sales skills (prospecting, cold calling, nurturing, engaging, presenting, negotiating, closing, etc.) and knowledge (product, marketers, trends, business, etc.) A salesperson can enact the exchange of value between a buyer and the vendor. Selling skills is yet another skill you weren't taught in school but it is a must-have skill in climbing up the ladder of your career. There is a constant need for value. Something must be sold whether tangible or intangible. People are always buying one thing or the other. Developing a sales career will require you to possess the specific skills needed to sell a product or service.

You'll suffer all manner of rejections by prospective customers throughout your career and so your skills require the following;

- **A high level of confidence**

    To be a great salesperson, you must have high confidence in yourself and your product or services. It is vital to have unwavering faith in yourself and the product you're pitching if you must make headways in sales. When transferred to the customer, this confidence in your product brings about trust and brand loyalty. If you lack confidence, you will do badly in selling. Graduates hoping to get into a career in sales must work at building their level of confidence.

- **Positivity**

After making your sales pitch and convincing them to purchase, you must be positive about the outcomes. The art of selling can be full of obstacles and as such you must have the belief to overcome any challenges thrown your way. Develop a positive attitude when going out for sales marketing.

- **Resilience**

Sales marketing could sometimes be very difficult as it might take long to convince a single client to purchase. You must be resilient as a salesperson to achieve your goals irrespective of the odds involved.

- **Communication skills**

You must be able to communicate the value of your product with conviction to your customer. Communicating with conviction can help transmit your passion for sales in an interview when applying for a sales job. One basic skill you must master when selling is communication. It is fundamental in building trust and creating a good rapport with the customers. In communicating, you get to know the customers' needs through active listening geared at proffering solutions.

- **Knowledge of the product**

You must know the product to be sold to convince prospective buyers easily. Without a good knowledge of the product, especially its benefit and competitive advantage, it might be difficult to convince the buyer.

- **Build a good rapport with the customers**

    This is important as you've got to convince them that you are the best person to sell them a product. It could begin with a kind gesture or compliment which will translate to a good relationship if developed.

- **Sell your personality**

    This is also valuable in developing your selling skills. People need to connect to your person before they can connect to what you offer. Sell a personality that can be trusted and relied on, sell a friendly personality so people can easily get to like your person. This will make buying from you a lot easier.

Building good selling skills as a graduate starting his/her career is a sure way to advance your career as good salespersons are always relevant in every organization. Every organization is out to make a profit by offering value, either by selling a product or rendering a service. For this reason, employers are keen on employing graduates with extraordinary selling skills that can be converted to profit. They look for the best salespersons that can help them meet their sales target per time. Any organization not meeting sales target is merely just operating but not advancing. One way you can break out from the competition is to develop a strong selling skill and with that, you can work in any organization and then grow from there.

Sometimes, employers hire salespersons intending to promote them if they do very well at selling or marketing, they can be transferred to other departments or given a higher responsibility. So, do not see selling as just a mere job, it is a crucial aspect of every organization, and people skilled at it rise to the upper echelon of their career. In selling, you offer more value to clients than simply selling an item. You increase your chances of being a great salesperson when you approach selling as solving a problem. You build a loyal and larger clientele base.

There is no better time to show these skills than in your job interview as this is the ultimate sale. Selling not just your talent but more importantly your personality. We're all in sales, in one form or another. How well you engage your selling skills makes a lot of difference.

Action Point

Seek to solve a problem when selling rather than merely making a profit. The latter sells you better.

12

ENTREPRENEURIAL SKILLS

"Entrepreneurship without skills limits your growth potential "Strive Masiyiwa.

FACTS AND STATS

1. According to the Global Entrepreneurship Monitor, the number of new businesses being started each year has been increasing 25% in recent years.

2. A survey by the Small Business Administration found that approximately 50% of small businesses fail within the first five years.

3. According to Fidelity Investments research, a 2021 study found that 88% of millionaires are self-made, with the remaining 12% having inherited significant money.

4. According to the World Bank, cash flow concerns are a major reason firms close their doors. In fact, 82% of small businesses report this as the primary cause for their demise.

5. There are 7 Women Entrepreneurs for Every 10 Male Entrepreneurs Starting a Business.

Most students and graduates often think they only require entrepreneurial skills if they intend to become entrepreneurs and set up their own business as graduates. They fail to realize that employers often seek an entrepreneurial mindset in their graduate recruits. This is so because they understand that graduates with entrepreneurial spirits can spot gaps in the market and innovate because they are commercial-minded. They have a growth mentality and the potentials to increase whatever they do.

Mark Cuban once said that children should be taught to be entrepreneurs because it will teach them several other important life skills but sadly, this is not so as most of our kids are taught to be lawyers or doctors. No one ever says "I want to be an entrepreneur. Parents fail to understand that succeeding in these other careers required some entrepreneurial qualities and abilities.

Today with the emergency of new industries and successful businesses, people now talk about entrepreneurs as the world is gradually tilting towards their direction. That is why it is a priority for fresh graduates to have this skill whether they intend to start their businesses or not. This skill will be required for career advancement. This skill will be necessary to scale up your dream and drive.

More than ever, employers are looking for entrepreneurial graduates because they become great assets to their company and organization. They are full of ideas that will advance the company. They are always looking for new and innovative ways of carrying out their task. Entrepreneurial recruits always look for opportunities for their organization that may further earn them a salary raise or promotion. Developing entrepreneurial skills that qualify you for that job involves effective communication and listening. They pay close attention to details and can identify new opportunities. Being entrepreneurial involves spotting an unexploited opportunity and making the most of it, especially, identifying a gap in the market and filling it. It could also involve trying something novel, improving a process efficiently, or boosting results.

Entrepreneurial skills are effectively a combination of other competencies which includes:

- **Commercial awareness**

    Entrepreneurs are always the first to know about trends in the market, identify opportunities to make commercial sales, and create awareness. Graduates with entrepreneurial skills are commercially driven. When they see an opportunity, they look for ways to create commercial awareness of the business.

- **Creative and innovative thinking**

Entrepreneurs are known to be creative and innovative thinkers. They are always looking for creative ways of advancing their business or giving a new outlook to an already existing idea. Having these sets of persons in your team of employees will give your company an advantage in the face of competition.

- **Problem-solving**

Entrepreneurs are problem solvers. Whenever they spot a problem, they proffer solutions through creative, logical, and analytical thinking.

- **Risk-taking**

One very profound trait of an entrepreneur is risk-taking. They are good at taking well-calculated risks for their business or organization as long as it is for a greater benefit and good.

- **Adaptability**

Entrepreneurs can adapt to changes in their environment whether economical or otherwise. They will always devise a means to adapt to whatever change they encounter in the evolving global market and industry.

- **Flexibility**

This trait allows entrepreneurs to cope with new trends and changes. They open their mind to new ideas. They are not rigid and do not fight change.

- **Leadership**

Building a successful business entails organizing people and resources to achieve set goals. Entrepreneurship involves effective leadership qualities and abilities. These qualities will enable you to face obstacles that may arise along the way.

- **Negotiation**

Entrepreneurs are very good negotiators. They know how to negotiate change and business deals for their organizations. They know what negotiating techniques to employ to get their desired outcome. This is why they are highly sought after by employers.

Here are a few ways you can develop your entrepreneurial skill to make you employable:

- **Set up a small business on the side**

In building your entrepreneurial skills, you can set up a side business aside from your degree to make some extra money. Nurture and grow that business while waiting to secure your dream job. Breaking the law of inertia to start a business is the most difficult stage of entrepreneurship. Converting your ideas into a tangible business with an entrepreneurial drive. Starting a small business goes beyond just having an idea. It encompasses all you need to do and put in place to ensure the business is off ideation stage to execution.

- **Be a voracious reader**

    Knowledge keeps you on the edge when doing business. What you know that your competitors don't know is what makes you stand out. This is only possible through reading and studying. Be a voracious reader. Know what is happening in your industry and other industries. Reading opens you up to several inherent opportunities in the business world. Read books that motivate your entrepreneurial drive and spirit. Also, read the biographies and autobiographies of entrepreneurs you admire. Watch TED talks about entrepreneurialism and innovation, read their stories and how they started, mistakes and pitfalls they encountered. This will enable you to avoid certain mistakes in your entrepreneurial journey.

- **Attend business pitches and seminars**

    Get into environments that challenge your entrepreneurial drive. Business pitches and seminars are good places to get inspired. Entrepreneurs need a lot of inspiration to get fresh ideas and sustain their innate entrepreneurial abilities and prowess.

- **Get mentors and role models in your fields**

    Look out for successful entrepreneurs in your field that you can access for mentorship and guide. This will better equip you for the journey ahead.

    Finally, you must be careful during interviews when your entrepreneurial skills are being tested through interview questions designed to access your entrepreneurial skills. You should take the opportunity to show off your entrepreneurial activities and achievements done wherever possible. That will automatically give you an advantage over other applicants who may also be qualified for the job.

Action Point

As the world evolves daily, entrepreneurship becomes the surest way to ensure lasting financial freedom. There is an urgent need to develop this skill to remain relevant in this time and age.

13

TEAM BUILDING SKILLS

"Talent wins games, but teamwork and intelligence win championships"- Michael Jordan.

FACTS AND STATS

1. Companies with a fully engaged workforce can generate 50 percent as much revenue and income.
2. Employee satisfaction improves by up to 50% when they are surrounded by colleagues with whom they are friendly, according to corporate team building data.
3. According to 86% of executives, a lack of teamwork is to blame for overall corporate failures.
4. Over 50% of employees have stayed at a company because they felt like part of a team.
5. 48% of HR specialists say that they successfully and efficiently run global teams remotely.

The nicest thing about teamwork is always having others by your side. Teambuilding skills are one of the fundamental skills employers look for and it's on the graduate recruiters' high priority list. Employers want to know that you can collaborate, influence, and compromise in such a way that sustains the workflow and ethics. Teamwork is all about operating smoothly and efficiently within a group.

Being able to demonstrate team building skills involves several abilities such as:

- **The ability to encourage and inspire other team members**

Team building involves encouraging and motivating others to perform optimally regardless of the work environment. Team members will naturally rely on the team leader to encourage and inspire them to be more and do more.

- **The ability to reach a compromise**

    In team building, you must be willing to reach a compromise when necessary for the good of your team members and the organization at large. Team building involves sacrifice. It may not be convenient for you then, but you may need to compromise for the greater well.

- **The ability to better understand your team member**

    You cannot effectively work with people without understanding their behaviors, actions, and responses. This understanding will help you know how to relate with your team members to avoid disagreement and so the organizational goals can be met.

- **The ability to influence and motivate others to work**

    Your impact as a team leader will be measured by how well you influence and motivate others to work. Team building involves influence and motivation at all levels to ensure smooth work operations.

Team building skills are vital for smooth operations in the work environment as you cannot work alone. Self-isolation may not be possible in a workplace so you should develop your team-building skills to work effectively with people.

Developing team-building skills relies heavily on your interpersonal skills and how well you have improved them. You must know how to relate with people from different spheres of life and social strata not just with people you are familiar with. Some jobs will even require you to work with strangers and foreigners. You must learn how to communicate and build social relationships with them so you do not hinder the workflow.

Team building is a high priority for most employers because they are interested in individuals who can bring different strengths to teams, not those who will slow down operations. Working with people with very high spirit and good team-building skills will hasten the job to be done. Some fresh graduates may be particularly good at monitoring or evaluating progress and others may be great at contributing brilliant new ideas. The organization achieves more when everyone's efforts are brought to the table. Less becomes more when you have so many hands-on decks. Team building skills enhance organizational survival and overall growth.

Team building skills are essential for conflict resolution in the workplace. While some people may not be able to understand others and why they act the way they do. People with good team-building skills will also be able to help solve organizational conflicts through simple dialogue and communication. When you take your time to study people, you will know what measures to employ when solving conflicts involving them.

Ways you can develop your team-building skills include;

- **Participate in group projects**

    You can develop your team-building skills by participating in group projects. When you do group projects you save time by getting the job done faster and have ample time to get to know your team members. Participating in a group project will teach you a couple of things: patience, connectivity, tolerance, flexibility, and adaptability. It's not easy working with people but as tough as it is, it builds your team-building skills.

- **Try to solve a puzzle with friends**

    You can also build this skill by trying to solve a puzzle with friends and see how well you demonstrate your team-building skills and adjust in areas where necessary.

- **Embrace the opportunity to work with others**

    An excellent place to build up team spirit is at sports clubs. Embrace every opportunity you get to work with others. Volunteering for a charity project will also allow you to build this skill as you will often be paired with others to reach a common goal.

- **Get internship space and part-time jobs**

    Internships and part-time jobs are good places to develop team-building skills because you will work with new people in a professional or corporate environment.

Team building skills and problem-solving skills go hand in hand. If you cannot work amicably with people, finding a solution to a problem in a team may be very difficult. This is why you must ensure a good and consistent rapport between you and your team members. Otherwise, problem-solving will take longer than necessary and you may even not come up with any solution. Your ability to successfully achieve that without much difficulty helps in team building. When a group works well together, it achieves the best results. Employers, therefore, want to hire people with team-building skills.

Good team builders can help groups work together well and meet their goals. Building and managing a successful team is a qualification for many jobs. If you're being considered for a position requiring managing or being part of a team, you must show that you have the team-building skills necessary for the job.

You must also explain your team-building skills on your CVs, graduate job application form, or at an interview. Emphasize how your contribution allowed the team to reach its full potential and achieve its goals. This will go a long way to show how well you have developed your team-building skills.

The four stages of team building development are:

- Forming: In this stage, team members are polite, cautious, and optimistic about the team's goals.
- Storming: In this stage, conflicts arise among team members and disagreements about roles and responsibilities may occur.
- Norming: In this stage, the team begins to work together more effectively and resolve conflicts.
- Performing: In this stage, the team becomes high performing and operates effectively and efficiently to accomplish its goals.

It's important to note that not all teams will necessarily go through all four stages, and some teams may cycle back to earlier stages at times. The goal is to reach the performing stage and maintain it through continuous communication, collaboration, and growth.

Action Point

You need people as much as you need the job. How well you develop your team-building skills will keep you longer on the job.

14

CV/RESUME WRITING SKILLS

"Packaging says it all'-

FACTS AND STATS

1. The average time spent by recruiters looking at a cv/resume: 5 to 7 seconds.
2. 76% of resumes are discarded for an unprofessional contact information especially phone numbers and email address.
3. Applicant Tracking Software, the robots that read your resume, are able to quickly eliminate 75% of the applicants.
4. 68% of employers will find you on social media platform such as Facebook, LinkedIn and Twitter.
5. 93% of recruiters are likely to look at a candidate's social media profile.

    A CV is a longer synopsis of your educational and academic background, teaching and research experience, publications, awards, presentations, honors, and additional details. It is a very important document that you must be skilled at developing and packaging. Some people even take it up as a career or business in corporate writing where they get paid for preparing CVs for people who can't do it themselves. Many fresh graduates usually find it difficult to prepare their CVs in such a way that it appeals to employers. It is either it's too scanty with vital details omitted or it's too lengthy with loads of unnecessary information it is.

    Every fresh graduate must learn to prepare their CVs to meet employers' professional standards. Your CV must emphasize your professional qualifications, education, experience, accomplishment, activities, and special qualifications if any. Often, graduates are so hurried to submit CVs that they fail to carefully arrange and package them. CV packaging skill is important for fresh graduates as it is the time in their lives when this skill will be tested more than ever.

Graduates recruiters expect that applicants know how to package their CVs to suit the position or type of job they are applying for. There are certain guidelines you must know when packaging a CV, a few are listed below:

- The order of topics in a CV format is flexible. There is no laid down order when arranging topics in a CV. It can follow any order you choose to use.

- Make it short and interesting. Don't make it more than two pages - nobody will want to read that. Usually, the hiring managers look through dozens of resumes and don't have time for long essays. Avoid clichés - they will make the CV less interesting.

- CV writing is not essay writing. You have to arrange sections highlighting strengths for the position you seek. You shouldn't start highlighting your strength in driving when applying for a teaching job. This is where most graduates make a mistake because they weren't taught in school. Your area of strength being highlighted should be those that match the position you are applying for.

- Your CV has to be clear and grammatically correct. Use positive language and industry-related words. Use them only if you are sure that they are applied in the right place.

- Divide the CV, so it has headings and subheadings. Try to avoid long paragraphs when talking about your skills, achievements, academic qualifications, etc. Use bullet points, so the manager will instantly see the things he needs to see.

CV/RESUME WRITING SKILLS

- Always elaborate and emphasize accomplishment and skills within the categories and these items listed within each category must be listed chronologically. That is the most recent appearing first.

- You may also need to include additional headings when appropriate to reflect your certifications, licenses, or workshop/training.

- Write about your hobby and interests and mention if you demonstrate leadership skills. Also, write about the voluntary work that you've done.

- Your CV must be packaged in a presentable and attractive style for easy access. Do not write your CV as though it's the story of your life. The laid down guidelines must be followed.

- Be easy to connect with. Always include your phone number and probably your LinkedIn username. Some employers tend to connect using it rather than to write e-mails. Give your e-mail address, but make sure it is professional, with your name and surname.

- Have a good knowledge of your industry. Show that you know what you are talking about. Do some research about the company and its employers? Then include your knowledge in the covering letter - talk about your weaknesses, strengths and mention what you can do to improve the company.

How you package your CV goes a long way to tell your employer how serious you are and how qualified you are for the job. It doesn't have to be too elaborate. It could be simple and concise but has all the relevant details. You may not necessarily need to go through rigorous interview processes if your CV speaks volumes of you and your qualifications.

CV/RESUME WRITING SKILLS

CV packaging skill is a skill that can be learnt if given careful attention. You'll exhume a great level of confidence when you appear before interviewers knowing you've thoroughly drafted your CV yourself.

Many graduates contract people to write their CVs for them which is not bad in itself but the inability to defend what is written is where the problem lies that is why it is most preferable to do it yourself. You could get templates online on how to write a professional CV and follow suit. It is no big deal.. All required is to follow the guidelines of writing a professional CV.

Another aspect of CV packaging where some fresh graduates make mistakes is sending the electronic versions of their CV for online job applications. When sending electronic versions, attach a file or simply cut and paste them into the text of the email message. You could also state your objectives and career interests in the first few lines of the email. Ensure to use language and acronyms recognized in your fields. Avoid using bold, italics, underlining lines, or graphics. Use all caps for emphasis.

To summarize, your CV should include the following. Your details, name, age (optional), address, phone number, and e-mail. They must be noticeable at first sight. Education and qualifications. Start from the highest, for example from university to courses, to work experience, if you have it and abilities.

A good CV is crucial for getting a job. However, while writing a CV, don't consider it a way to get a job. A good CV is a way to get you to the interview.

Avoid these resume mistakes!

- Choosing education over experience.
- A resume should not be tailored to a specific application.
- Instead of the executive summary, outline career objectives.
- Uncertain achievements.
- Insufficient research.

15 Free Websites to Build your Resume or CV

With so many tools available online, creating a resume or CV has never been easier. A resume builder is an online application or piece of software that provides users with interactive forms and templates for quickly and easily creating a resume.

An excellent resume builder does not simply provide you with a generic template and fill it with generic information; instead, it takes the time to craft a tailored resume to increase your chances of getting hired.

Not all resume builders offer the same tools for creating your resume.

Without further ado, here are 15 sites that can help you write and package your resume or CV in no particular order.

1. Indeed: Offers a free resume builder and access to thousands of job postings.
2. LinkedIn: Lets you create a professional profile and includes a resume builder feature.

CV/RESUME WRITING SKILLS

3. Zety: An AI-powered resume builder that offers personalized suggestions and a wide range of pre-made templates.
4. Novoresume: Offers a user-friendly resume builder with a wide range of templates.
5. Resume.com: Allows you to create a free resume and cover letter with a variety of templates.
6. VisualCV: Offers an online resume builder with a wide range of templates and customization options.
7. MyPerfectResume: An online resume builder with a vast library of professionally written bullet points and job descriptions.
8. Resume-Builder: A user-friendly website that offers customizable templates, a step-by-step resume builder, and tips and advice on resume writing.
9. ResumeMaker - A resume builder that offers templates, expert advice, and a step-by-step guide to help you create a professional-looking resume.
10. Resume Genius: A resume builder that offers expert tips, advice, and templates to help you create a professional-looking resume.
11. Novoresume: A modern resume builder that offers AI-powered suggestions and pre-made templates.
12. Canva: A graphic design platform that offers customizable resume templates and drag-and-drop design tools.
13. Resume-Now: A user-friendly resume builder that offers step-by-step guidance and pre-made templates.

14. Resumonk - An online resume builder that offers pre-made templates, a drag-and-drop interface, and easy-to-use design tools.

15. ResumeHelp: An online resume builder that offers a wide range of customizable templates, tips and advice, and a step-by-step guide to help you create a winning resume.

Action Point

Package your CV the way you want employers to perceive you.

15

BUSINESS PLAN WRITING SKILLS

"Good business planning is 9 parts execution for every 1 part strategy." – Tim Berry

FACTS AND STATS
1. Entrepreneurs who have their business plans were 50% likely to succeed in growing their business than those who do not have.
2. A study found that both the written business plan and the process of business planning "augment" the firm's performance.
3. 82% of businesses fail because of cash flow mismanagement and this cab attributed to lack of business plan.
4. Start-Ups that write formal business plan receive more formal financial support than if they had no plan, according to a 2019 study.
5. 69% of venture capitalists say that they have not invested in new ventures without reviewing a business plan first.

Developing business plan writing skills as a fresh graduate is a valuable asset for your future career. A well-written business plan can help secure funding, attract investors, and guide the overall success of a business. Here are some steps you can take to improve your business plan writing skills:

- Study Business Plan Basics: Familiarize yourself with the basic elements of a business plan, including executive summary, company description, market analysis, product or service offerings, marketing and sales strategies, financial projections, and executive management.

- Read Examples: Read as many business plans as possible to see how they are structured and what information they contain. This will give you a good idea of what works and what doesn't. You can find business plans online, in books, and in business plan competitions.

- Take Courses: Consider taking courses or workshops that focus on business planning, entrepreneurship, or writing in general. These courses can help you gain knowledge and skills in a structured environment.

- Network with Business Owners: Talk to business owners and entrepreneurs to learn about their experiences and get their perspectives on what makes a successful business plan. Ask them to review your drafts and provide feedback.

- Write, Rewrite, and Revise: Writing a business plan is a process, and it's likely that you'll need to revise and refine your plan several times before it's complete. Don't be discouraged if your first draft isn't perfect; just keep working on it until you're satisfied with the final product.

- Get Feedback: Seek feedback from people you trust, such as mentors, peers, or experienced business consultants and professionals. They can help you identify areas that need improvement and suggest changes that will strengthen your plan.

Let's take a look at the 10 Components of a business plan

1. **Executive Summary:** The executive summary of a business plan is a condensed version of the entire plan that provides a brief overview of the key points and goals of a proposed business venture. It is usually written last, after the rest of the plan has been developed, and serves as an introduction to the plan for potential investors, lenders, or stakeholders. The executive summary which normally a 1 - 2 page

document should include the purpose of the business, the target market, the products or services offered, the business strategy and structure, financial requirement and projections, and the management team. The main goal of the executive summary is to grab the reader's attention and convince them to continue reading the full plan. It should be well-written, clear, and concise, and effectively communicate the potential of the business.

2. **Market Analysis:** Market analysis is a crucial part of a business plan that provides information and thorough analysis about the target market, customer demographics, buying habits, competition, and economic trends. It helps businesses to understand the demand for their products or services and identify opportunities and challenges in the market.

The market analysis typically includes the following elements:

- Industry analysis: An overview of the industry in which the business operates and its current trends.

- Target market: A description of the specific group of customers the business is targeting.

- Competitor analysis: An evaluation of the business's direct and indirect competitors and their strengths and weaknesses.

- Market size: An estimate of the potential market size and growth rate.

- Market trends: An analysis of current and future market trends, such as changes in consumer behavior and technology.

The market analysis provides valuable information that helps businesses to make informed decisions and develop effective strategies to compete in the market.

3. **Competitive Analysis:** Competitive analysis is the process of evaluating the strengths and weaknesses of competitors in order to develop a business strategy that differentiates your business and improves its competitiveness. In the context of a business plan, a competitive analysis provides information on the competition's products, services, market position, target customer segments, and marketing strategies.

   Furthermore, using a SWOT Analysis which is a strategic planning tool enables an organization to identify strengths, weaknesses, opportunities, and threats to help guide decision-making and identify potential risks and growth areas. This information can help you determine how to position your own business to differentiate it from competitors, identify opportunities to capture new market share, and make informed decisions about pricing, product development, and marketing strategies.

4. **Product or Service Line:** This section is where you provide a detailed description of the products or services that your business will offer. This section should include the following information:

   Product or service description: Provide a clear and concise description of what your business will offer. Explain the features and benefits of your products or services and how they are different from what is currently available in the market.

- Target market: Identify your target market, including demographic information and specific needs that your products or services will address.

- Pricing strategy: Describe your pricing strategy, including how you will determine the prices for your products or services and how they compare to those of your competitors.

- Production plan: If you are offering physical products, provide a production plan that outlines how you will manufacture and distribute your products.

5. **Marketing and Sales Strategies:** Marketing and sales strategies are critical components of a business plan as they outline how a company intends to reach and retain customers, generate revenue and achieve its overall goals. Marketing strategies focus on identifying target audiences, promoting products/services, and building brand awareness through advertising, digital marketing, direct sales, trade shows, referrals, public relations, word of mouth, distribution channels and other tactics.

    Sales strategies, on the other hand, focus on closing deals and generating revenue by targeting specific segments, establishing partnerships, and leveraging technology and tools to streamline the sales process. Both marketing and sales strategies should be aligned with the company's overall goals and objectives and regularly reassessed to ensure they remain relevant and effective.

6. **Operations Plan:** A description of the day-to-day processes and systems needed to run the business, including manufacturing or service delivery, staffing

requirements and formulating policies and procedures that help run the business cost-effectively.

The operations plan is the section of your business plan that provides an overview of your workflow, supply chains, and other similar business aspects. It should also include information about any physical plants, equipment, assets, and general operational details that will assist investors in understanding the physical details of your vision.

It may also include information about inventory requirements, suppliers, quality control, and a description of the manufacturing process, certifications and licenses depending on the type of business you'll be running.

It can also be used as a checklist for startups, outlining everything that must be done in order to begin turning a profit.

7. **Team and Management Plan**: This section of a business plan is where you provide information about key personnel involved in the company, their background, and their responsibilities. This section is important as it shows potential investors and stakeholders the experience and expertise of the people behind the business and their ability to execute the business plan. It typically includes brief overview of the key personnel involved in the business, relevant skills, their roles, and responsibilities.

- An organizational structure (Organogram) which is a diagram or chart that shows the company's hierarchy, including the names and positions of key personnel may be required.

- Personnel plan: An overview of the company's personnel plan, including the number of employees, their roles and responsibilities, and compensation - salaries and wages plans.

- Advisory board: Information about any advisors or board members and their relevant experience and expertise.

8. **Organizational Structure:** A description of the formal structure of the business, including ownership and management hierarchies. It refers to the formal framework that defines the relationships between different components of an organization, such as departments, teams, roles, and responsibilities. It provides a clear chain of command, outlines the responsibilities of each position, and helps to ensure that everyone knows who to report to and who is responsible for what.

   Organizational structure is important as it helps to ensure clear communication, efficient decision-making, and effective delegation of responsibilities within an organization.

9. **Financial Plans and Projections:** The "Financial Plans and Projections" section of a business plan is where you present the financial data and assumptions that support the viability of your business. This section is critical for demonstrating to investors and lenders that your business has the potential to generate sufficient revenue and profit to repay loans and provide a return on investment.

   It typically includes the following information:

   - **Sales and revenue projections:** A projection of sales and revenue over a period of time, based on your market research, marketing strategies, and pricing strategies.

- **Cost projections:** A projection of the costs associated with operating your business, including labor costs, materials, and overhead expenses.

- **Gross profit margin:** A calculation of the gross profit margin, which is the difference between revenue and cost of goods sold, expressed as a percentage of revenue.

- **Operating expenses:** A projection of the costs associated with running the business, including rent, utilities, salaries, and other operating expenses.

- **Net profit or loss:** A calculation of the net profit or loss, which is the difference between revenue and all expenses.

- **Break-even analysis:** A calculation of the point at which the business is expected to cover all its costs and begin to generate a profit.

- **Projected cash flow:** A projection of the inflow and outflow of cash for the business over a period of time, including expected sources of income, and expected payments for expenses.

- **Projected balance sheet:** A projection of the business's assets, liabilities, and equity at a given point in time.

   Financial projections are based on a set of assumptions, and it's important to note that actual results may differ from the projections.

10. **Appendix and Supporting Documents.** This section of a business plan is an optional section that can be included to provide additional information or

supporting evidence to the main body of the business plan.

This section typically includes the following:

- Resumes of key personnel: Detailed resumes of the key personnel involved in the business, including their background, education, experience, and achievements.

- Supporting documents: Any additional documents that support the information presented in the business plan, such as contracts, letters of reference, or market research reports.

- Legal documents: Any legal documents related to the business, such as articles of incorporation, bylaws, or licenses.

- Strategic partnership and alliances: This is a contract between two or more organizations to work together on a particular business activity in order for each to capitalize on the advantages of the other and gain a competitive edge.

- Technical specifications: Detailed information about ay technical specifications or designs related to the product or service offered by the business.

The appendix section is not necessary for every business plan, but it can be useful for providing additional information and context to support the viability of the business.

As a fresh graduate, developing business plan writing skills takes time and effort, but the benefits are well worth it. By following these steps, you can gain the knowledge and skills necessary to create a compelling and effective business plan that will help you achieve your goals for you and your organization.

Action Point

A business plan is like a blueprint that helps you articulate what you have in mind and where you want to go; it drives you to determine the best way to get there.

Every idea is realizable, start by transferring it from an intangible form to a tangible form using ink on paper.

16

TIME MANAGEMENT SKILLS

"Time management is life management" - Robin Sharma

FACTS AND STATS

1. Almost half (49%) of people have never carried out a time audit to understand how they spend their time.

2. On the average the professional spends around 2 hours a day on social media and other digital activities that sums to 50% of workplace distraction.

3. Up to 80% of employees say that chatty coworkers are the reason for a lack of focus on the job.

4. On average, people "waste" 1 and a 1/2 hours (91 minutes) each day on tasks and meetings that aren't important to their role.

5. 75% of staff say they are more productive after attending time management training for distractions at work.

Time is a valuable asset everyone has in life. How well you spend it is directly proportional to the results you get in life. Until you can manage time, you cannot manage anything else. Life is measured in time and how well you spend your 24hours every day will determine what your life will become years later. The truth is nobody is too busy, it's just a matter of priorities. You obviously will give more time to the things that are of utmost priority to you.

Employers across several rapidly growing industries very value time management and scheduling skills. The ability to effectively manage time is a highly attractive in a job candidate. Time management is a planning process dedicated to making the best use of your working hours.

Employers want to save time and get more jobs done. Therefore, they won't go for a time waster but a good time manager. How well do you manage your time? While you try to answer that question, understand that effective time management requires you to plan your day. Which is what a lot of people don't do. When you are not prepared for something, you'll fall for anything. When you fail to plan your day, you allow unnecessary activities to steal your time while those of top priorities suffer. This is why it is important to brace up your time management skills as you will be required to do a couple of tasks in a stipulated time. How frequently do you meet deadlines?

Timing and scheduling are keys to productivity in all aspects of life. By assigning time to every activity, you function optimally. Managing time will enable you to achieve maximum productivity, avoid rushing to meet deadlines, and allot in free time for unforeseen engagements and commitments.

Here, are a few ways you can effectively manage your time for optimal productivity in your workplace;

- **Do regular self-assessment**

    One way you can evaluate yourself if you have good time management skills is through self-assessment. It is vital to determine whether you have good time management skills. You must learn how to evaluate your habits and patterns to know how they impact your productivity at work. And if there are areas that do, you need to readjust. Habits like oversleeping can impact negatively your time management skills. Ensure you carry out regular self-assessment, know what activities consume the greater part of your time. People often spend the best of their time online, chit-chatting, liking posts and comments. By doing self-assessment, you'll be able to identify your major time consumer. If it doesn't advance your life and career, you should redress. And channel the better part of your time in your job and impacting your life positively.

TIME MANAGEMENT SKILLS

- **Assign a time to every task**

    Good time management begins with knowing how much time you have to do a task. This may vary depending on the work environment, customer's needs, and other peculiarities of the task. However, knowing what time is needed to finish a task is essential when building good time management skills. Assigning a time to every task helps you finish up within a stipulated time. Employees see effective time managers as a very important part of their workflow.

- **Learn to say 'NO'**

    Learning to say 'NO' politely to certain unplanned activities and persons that may try to thwart your efforts to manage your time wisely. Letting everyone encroach into your scheduled time may hamper your desired results for the day. It is not wrong to say no to activities, not in your schedule. Never accept new commitments when you already have too much on your schedule. It inhibits effective time management. Taking up tasks you can finish within a given schedule will aid time management.

- **Examine your work patterns**

    Occasionally examine your work patterns to assess your skill set. If you discover that you often rush to complete your work during a typical workday with no additional time between the end of one task and the start of another, you may not be managing your time properly. Most often, plans do not always go according to schedule and we must adjust. But if you find out that you are consistently taking longer than expected to finish a task, it may be a sign that your time management skills need to be refined.

- **Plan your daily schedule**

    Planning is very necessary for time management. You may need to draw up a daily schedule of your activities to help you manage your time. In drafting this plan, know what is to be done, and what follows. Time scheduling apps are available as phone apps that help you plan a schedule. You should check it out.

    Good time management skills will empower you to be the best version of your professional self. You may find it difficult to create a healthy work-life balance when you cannot manage your time. When you do not have enough time to carry out your activities, know that you are not effectively managing your time. Time is constant but your work pattern may change. know how to master your time even when work pattern changes.

    Building good time management skills shows how valuable you are in the workplace and serves you as an individual. People value you and your time when they know you are good at managing your time. When you intentionally manage your time, you invest wisely in yourself and your goals. Every investor is entitled to his\her reward.

    What are you investing your time in? For fresh graduates, you should invest your time in personal development, building networks, reading, learning soft skills, and engaging in other productive activities that can improve your career pursuits. Fresh graduates who are good time managers show respect for their own time and the time of their employers as well. Knowing how to effectively manage your time enables you to be more efficient at work, creating positive outcomes for your personal and professional lives.

Lastly, know that time management is tested throughout the recruitment process. One of the most obvious ways is through assessing how you conduct yourself throughout the process. For example, when you submit your application, no recruiter expects you to get an application in within the first 12 hours after a position has been advertised. That would suggest that you haven't taken the time to reflect on and tailor your CV to suit the application. Also, when reviewing our CV or application form, employers will judge your ability to manage your time by looking at whether you have fitted in part-time jobs and extracurricular activities alongside your studies. This will show if you can manage your time effectively on the job.

Action Point

Time is an investment. The difference between yours and mine is what we choose to invest our time in.

17

EMOTIONAL INTELLIGENCE SKILLS

"If your emotional abilities aren't in hand if you don't have self-awareness if you are not able to manage your distressing emotions if you can't have empathy and have effective relationships, then no matter how smart you are, you are not going to get very far'- Daniel Goleman.

FACTS AND STATS

1. Emotional intelligence is one of the top 10 most sought-after skills and is expected to remain so through 2025 and beyond.
2. Studies have shown that EI is a strong predictor of job performance, accounting for up to 90% of the differences in how successful people are in their careers.
3. 64% of emotionally intelligent companies have a high degree of empowerment and tolerance for risk.
4. 82% of global companies use EQ tests for executive positions, 72% for middle management, and 59% for entry-level positions.
5. At a Motorola manufacturing plant, 93% of employees became more productive after the facility adopted stress-reduction and emotional-intelligence programs.

In the words of Travis Bradberry, emotional intelligence is your ability to recognize and understand emotions in yourself and others, and the ability to use this awareness to manage your behavior and relationships. Having strong emotional intelligence as a fresh graduate begins with understanding and gaining mastery over your own emotions. You cannot demonstrate emotional intelligence in a situation that requires it when you do not know your basic emotional reactions, behaviors, responses, and attitudes.

Daniel Goleman puts it this way *"if you are tuned out of your own emotions, you will be poor at reading them in other people"*. This invariably means that emotional intelligence is first about understanding personal emotions. Emotional intelligence, also called EI or EQ, is the ability to identify and deal with our emotions, recognize and understand the feelings, and adjust our behavior and responses to others accordingly. Emotional intelligence helps boost self-awareness, self-control, motivation, empathy, and social skills, all of which help us become a much better heroes.

Emotional intelligence can help graduates become the best at what they do. Be the best colleague possible and achieve career success. When developing emotional intelligence skills for your career and professional life, some vital components of other skills will be brought to bear. Some of which are;

- **Self-knowledge**

    When you understand your emotional makeup, it will be easy to relate to others. Having a good knowledge of yourself will help you know how to control and keep your emotions in check.

- **Empathy**

    This is the ability to put yourself in the shoes and situations of others to better interact with them. Empathizing with others will enable you to know how to respond to their emotional needs.

- **Communication skills**

    Your ability to effectively interact and communicate your thoughts with various people will determine how well you've developed your emotional intelligence skills. Building good communication skills will in no little way impact your emotional intelligence skills.

- **Interpersonal relationship**

    Developing sound emotional intelligence skills will require you to possess interpersonal skills. Those are those skills that enable you to communicate effectively. Your emotional intelligence will be impaired when you cannot use your interpersonal skills which include; active listening, dependability, responsibility, leadership, etc.

Emotional intelligence skills are crucial to exhibit in the workplace as you will deal with many people with varying emotional responses. Listed below are what your emotional intelligence skills will do for you in your workplace:

- Developing emotional intelligence skills can help you build better relationships and make things run smoothly in the workplace. For instance, if you want to request a colleague you suspect is feeling down, how and when you make your request should be different from what it would be when the person is in a good state.

- Emotional intelligence will help you understand how people react. Most especially, to changes and that knowledge will enable you to choose a more appealing approach.

- It enhances your persuasion skills. If you need to persuade a client to take a certain course of action that they have doubts about, understanding what tickles their fancy will likely improve your chances of success. You need to be highly emotionally intelligent to persuade people.

- It makes teamwork easier to accomplish. When you have a good knowledge of the emotional responses of your colleagues and people around you, you'll relate better with them, making teamwork easier and void of misunderstanding.

- It improves your ability to influence others. You cannot successfully influence people without a low emotional intelligence quotient. Knowing how people react to different situations will help you better influence them. You can easily tell what gets them to the peak of their game and what turns them off.

- Emotional intelligence skill plays an important role in a well-balanced and productive workplace as well as in leadership. In leading people, you must get involved in their lives and often engage with them to achieve the organization's collective goals. Strong emotional intelligence skills will help you become a successful and effective leader.

- Emotional intelligence skills when developed can be a good asset for a customer service or client management career. You work better as a customer service personnel when you learn to manage your emotions.

- Emotional intelligence can also improve your work performance and productivity because if you understand your emotions you can tell when you are stressed or not at your best. You could take steps to relieve the cause of the stress, rearrange your day to leave more complicated tasks to a better time.

Furthermore, you should know that when assessed during recruitment, employers won't judge how emotionally intelligent you are. They will probably be explicitly assessing your communication, teamwork, and relationship-building skills. All of which are enhanced by higher degrees of emotional intelligence. Peradventure you have a poor emotional intelligence quotient skill, you can improve it by interacting with different people from various backgrounds. Learn to work even with different people.

People with a higher emotional intelligence quotient can see things from other people's point of view, even if they don't agree with them. The best way to get started is by attending social functions and activities to meet other people and learn how they think. Also, volunteering and travelling can widen your horizon about people and read news and opinion pieces from various sources, particularly those you don't agree with. It helps you see things from other's perspectives and better understand why people might think differently from yours.

The most important aspect of emotional intelligence is getting to know yourself and how you think. Learn to recognize your triggers for stress or any negative behavior and develop strategies for avoiding them to be emotionally stable and balanced.

Action Point

Emotional intelligence is paramount when dealing with people. As you learn to develop it, you get better at interacting.

18

CREATIVITY AND INNOVATION SKILL

"Creativity is thinking up new things, innovation is doing new things"- Theodore Levitt

FACTS AND STATS

1. The majority of individuals particularly in the corporate world, 75% believe they have not realized their full creative and innovative potential.

2. About 60% of CEOs polled cited creativity as the most important leadership quality, compared with 52% for integrity and 35% for global thinking

3. 72% of Fortune 500 companies admit to have missed crucial growth opportunities and 60% struggle to learn from past mistakes.

4. Research shows that creative abilities can be enhanced through regular engagement in creative activities and exposure to diverse stimuli.

5. Stress negatively impacts creative expression, particularly when it involves rigid timeframes and criteria.

With the increasing number of fresh graduates leaving school every year, the need to be a step ahead of your equals through creativity and innovation will do you great good. Different graduate professions require creativity and innovation in different ways. That is why they employ not just those who seem qualified for the job but those with an extra advantage of being creative and innovative thinkers.

While creativity is the thoughts and vision of a new product or a different take on an existing product, innovation is an improved way of doing things. Employers like to have creative and innovative thinkers in their graduate hires as they come up with the ideas, big and small, that help their businesses succeed. Graduates who are creative and innovative stand a better chance to get picked for the job than those who are not.

CREATIVITY AND INNOVATION SKILL

Creativity and innovation skills are an integral part of other competencies and qualities. These other qualities include:

- **Problem-solving**

    Creativity is largely required in solving problems. You would need to be able to think thoroughly through the problem to come up with a creative or innovative approach to solving the problem. Many employees will jeopardize their chances of finding solutions to problems when they fail to employ creative and innovative graduates.

- **Entrepreneurial mindset**

    Creativity and innovation are the fundamental elements needed to thrive as an entrepreneur. Being creative opens your mind to new opportunities and innovation helps you improve on the identified opportunities.

- **Ability to adapt easily to new situations**

    The end product of every creative move is to discover new trends and situations and the ability to find ways to easily adapt to them shows how innovative you are.

- **Curiosity**

    Curiosity leads to creativity and innovation. It is your curious mind that drives you to be creative. So, keep your mind alert to produce creative or innovative ideas to stay current with trends.

CREATIVITY AND INNOVATION SKILL

- **Imagination**

    Creativity begins from within. It is your imaginary eyes you need to engage in creative thinking. Once you can imagine it, you can create it. Imagination brings your thoughts, ideas, and feelings from the intangible to the tangible.

- **Vision**

    Creative people are visionaries. Once their gaze is fixed on an idea or thing, they do everything possible to birth it. Having a vision for yourself will enhance your creativity and innovation. Vision is what drives you from one level to another. Graduates desiring to develop their creative skills must have a clear vision for their life and what they do.

    You may not attain certain heights in your career pursuits if you fail to think creatively or develop innovative ideas that can change the status of your organization. You will merely remain in the ordinary class, not the class exclusively for creative. Creativity and innovation, make you stand out in a class of your own. Graduates who are skilled creative can function in any job as long as it requires their brain to think and produce meaningful concepts.

    Professionals in different careers call upon their creativity in different ways. That is why we have creative directors in a company as they are responsible for designing creative approaches and concepts that will improve the organization and solve a problem. Graduates possessing these relevant skills will be sought after in different careers such as architecture, product design, web design, graphics, media, marketing, and advertising as diverse opportunities will be presented to them. Their creative prowess will be required in charting a new course or problem-solving. Management consultants need creative thinking to devise strategies for clients and sell these strategies most compellingly.

As creativity can be applied differently in different professions, recruiters may not explicitly stipulate creativity as an essential criterion for job descriptions. They'll be wrapped in the skills mentioned earlier and examined with those skills. Recruiters are looking for graduates with innovative problem-solving approaches so that growth is not impaired. You can start developing your creativity and innovation skills today by becoming active in running new organizations and creating your own blog, website, or app.

New organizations are a good breeding ground to start being creative. You'll need to develop fresh and new ideas for everything. Ranging from vision statements to business development strategies. All of these will require being creative and innovative to achieve. Graduates interested in writing or IT-related jobs such as creating blogs and websites will need a lot of creativity. Writing is one way that opens up your mind for creative thinking. Creativity will make your write-ups, materials, and articles preferable compared with others. Creativity gives beauty to your ideas when you write. It has a way of amplifying your thoughts and ideas.

Also, getting a part-time job as a tutor or teacher will improve your creative and innovative skills as lesson planning requires creativity and innovation. You will easily get bored of the classroom environment if you are not creative. Aside from employing creativity and innovation in lesson planning, it is most important during lessons or teaching. The teacher is expected to be able to come up with innovative ideas that will sustain the attention of the kids when learning. This is why many teachers, especially in nursery schools, often sing, dance, clap, and jump during lessons. All of these are to continuously make the kids interested in the lessons and to improve the memorability of the lessons.

The need to be creative and innovative in this time and day cannot be overemphasized because these are skills you must develop to move with the world as it evolves. Creativity keeps you alert and thinking. If you want your brain cells to stink, stop thinking and being innovative. Variety they say is the spice of life. Without creativity, there cannot be variety. You will appreciate the beauty of life when your mind can create like God, the ultimate creator.

Creative and innovative people can devise new ways to carry out tasks, solve problems, and meet challenges. They bring a fresh, and sometimes unorthodox, perspective to their work. This thinking can help departments and organizations move in more productive directions. For these reasons, they are extremely valuable to a company. Some people are naturally more creative than others, but creative thinking abilities can be learned.

If someone in your industry is known for being creative, you could connect with that person and ask for an informational interview, or ask to job shadow him or her for a day. Watching someone work in creative ways can help you learn to be more creative yourself.

Power of Questions

Power questions in creativity are questions that help to spark new ideas and perspectives, challenge assumptions, and encourage divergent thinking. Some examples of power questions in creativity include:

- What if we approached this problem from a completely different angle?

- How might we use this challenge as an opportunity for growth and innovation?
- What would happen if we combined two seemingly unrelated ideas or concepts?
- How might we push the boundaries of what is currently possible in this field?
- What if we inverted the traditional approach to this problem?
- How can we use our failures as a stepping stone for success?
- What would happen if we took a chance and tried something truly unconventional?
- These questions can help facilitate creative thinking and problem-solving by opening up new avenues of thought and encouraging individuals to consider innovative solutions.

Action Point

If your mind can think it, you can create it or improve on that already exists.

19

SOCIAL MEDIA/DIGITAL MARKETING SKILL

"Ignoring online marketing is like opening a business but not telling anyone." - KB Marketing Agency

FACTS AND STATS

1. As of January 2023, there are approximately 4.76 billion active social media users worldwide. The number is expected to reach nearly 5.42 billion by 2025.
2. The average user time on social networks is 2hr 25min, and more seniors aged 65+ are expected to join social media platforms by 2023.
3. Despite men making up the majority of social network users at 54.3%, it is women who spend more time on social media browsing.
4. In terms of digital marketing, it's estimated that businesses across the globe will spend over $435 billion on digital advertising in 2023.
5. Content creation and marketing are popular form of digital marketing, with over 70% of businesses reporting that they have a content marketing strategy in place.

The digital age has revolutionized the way businesses and brands reach their target audience. In today's world, having a strong digital marketing and social media presence is essential for any organization to thrive. As a fresh graduate looking to enter the workforce, developing digital marketing and social media skills can be the key to landing your dream job and building a successful career or business.

Developing digital marketing and social media skills allow professionals and businesses to reach a wider audience and target specific demographics, such as age, location, interests, and behaviors. It also allows for real-time monitoring and measurement of marketing campaigns, making it easier for businesses to track the effectiveness of their strategies and make adjustments as needed.

SOCIAL MEDIA/DIGITAL MARKETING SKILL

Digital marketing and social media are ever-evolving field, so it's important to stay current with the latest trends and best practices. Follow industry blogs, attend webinars and conferences, and take online courses to continuously improve your skills.

In this chapter, we will explore some crucial aspects of digital marketing and social media skills that can help you stay ahead of the curve.

- **Content Creation**

Content creation is one of the most critical aspects of digital marketing and social media. As a fresh graduate, it is essential to have the ability to create compelling content that resonates with your target audience. This includes writing blogs, social media posts, and creating engaging visuals such as videos and infographics. To excel in content creation, you should have a deep understanding of your target audience's interests, pain points, and preferences.

- **SEO**

Search Engine Optimization (SEO) is the process of optimizing your website or social media profiles to rank higher in search engine results pages (SERPs). SEO is a fundamental skill for digital marketers, as it enables your content to be easily found by your target audience. As a fresh graduate, it is essential to have a basic understanding of how SEO works and how to optimize content for search engines.

- **Social Media Management**

Social media management involves creating, scheduling, and publishing content on various social media platforms such as Facebook, Instagram, Twitter, and LinkedIn. As a digital marketer, you should have a good understanding of the various social media platforms and their unique features. Social media management also includes responding to comments and messages and analyzing social media metrics to determine the effectiveness of your social media strategy.

- **Email Marketing**

Email marketing is a cost-effective way to reach out to potential and existing customers. As a fresh graduate, you should know how to create effective email campaigns that drive engagement and conversions. This includes creating compelling subject lines, writing engaging content, and incorporating visuals such as images and videos. Interestingly, email marketing has the highest ROI out of all of these digital marketing skills. An incredible 4000% Return-On-Investment. Nothing on this list can beat that.

- **Basic Design Skills**

As a fresh graduate, there are several ways you can develop basic design skills. One approach is to enroll in online courses or tutorials that cover graphic design fundamentals such as typography, color theory, and layout design. You can also practice designing graphics and layouts using free design tools such as Canva and Adobe Spark. Additionally, you can seek feedback and guidance from experienced designers or join design communities to learn from other designers. With consistent practice and a willingness to learn, you can develop the basic design skills needed to create visually compelling digital content that effectively communicates your brand message.

- **Copywriting Skills**

As a fresh graduate, there are several ways you can develop copywriting skills. One approach is to read and analyze copywriting examples from successful brands and campaigns. This can help you understand the key elements of persuasive and compelling copy, such as the use of emotional appeals, strong headlines, and clear calls-to-action. You can also practice writing copy for different formats such as social media posts, email marketing, and landing pages. Additionally, seeking feedback and guidance from experienced copywriters or joining writing communities can help you improve your skills. By consistently practicing and refining your copywriting skills, you can create engaging and effective content that resonates with your target audience.

- **Affiliate Marketing**

Affiliate marketing can be done through various channels such as website banners, text links, email marketing, and social media. The affiliate and the business both benefit from this arrangement - the business gets exposure to a new audience, and the affiliate earns money for promoting the business's products or services.

Affiliate marketing is often used by online retailers, but it can also be used by other types of businesses such as service providers and information product creators. It's an effective way for businesses to reach a wider audience, and for affiliates to earn money by promoting products they believe in. Overall, affiliate marketing is a win-win relationship between businesses and affiliates, where both parties benefit from the marketing efforts of the other.

- **Data Analytics**

    Data analytics involves the collection, analysis, and interpretation of data to make informed decisions. As a digital marketer, you should have a good understanding of data analytics to track your website and social media performance. This includes using tools such as Google Analytics to track website traffic, bounce rates, and user behavior. You should also be able to analyze social media metrics such as engagement rates, follower growth, and reach.

- **Paid Advertising**

    Paid advertising involves placing ads on various platforms such as Google, Facebook, and LinkedIn to reach your target audience. As a fresh graduate, you should have a good understanding of how paid advertising works and how to create effective ads that drive conversions. This includes understanding the different ad formats, setting up ad campaigns, and analyzing the effectiveness of your ads.

- **Influencer Marketing**

    Influencer marketing involves partnering with influential people on social media to promote your brand or product. As a digital marketer, you should have a good understanding of how influencer marketing works and how to identify the right influencers for your brand. This includes understanding the different types of influencers, such as micro-influencers and macro-influencers, and analyzing their engagement rates and followers.

- **Mobile Optimization**

   With the rise of mobile devices, it is essential to optimize your website and social media profiles for mobile users. Mobile optimization involves creating a user-friendly experience that is optimized for the small screens and limited input capabilities of mobile devices. This includes having a responsive design that automatically adjusts to different screen sizes and mobile-friendly features such as easy navigation, quick loading times, and clear calls-to-action.

   Mobile optimization is critical for digital marketers because mobile devices have become the primary way people access the internet. In fact, according to Statista, mobile devices accounted for over 60% of all website traffic worldwide in 2023. This means that if your website or social media profiles are not optimized for mobile, you may be missing out on a significant portion of your target audience.

   To optimize for mobile, you should start by creating a responsive design that adapts to different screen sizes. This means that your website or social media profiles should be easy to navigate, load quickly, and have clear calls-to-action. You should also use mobile-friendly features such as click-to-call buttons and mobile-friendly forms to make it easy for users to interact with your brand on their mobile devices.

   In conclusion, digital marketing and social media skills are essential for fresh graduates looking to build a successful career in today's digital age. To excel in this field, you should have a strong foundation in content creation, SEO, social media management, email marketing, data analytics, paid advertising, influencer marketing, branding, mobile optimization, and continuous learning. By mastering these ten aspects of digital marketing and social media, you can build a strong digital presence for your brand and stay ahead of the curve in this rapidly evolving industry.

Action Point

Never before has competition been so fierce in the business world. With the evolution of technology, consumers can switch to a competitor in seconds. So strive to not only market but to inform our customers.

20

PERSONAL FINANCIAL MANAGEMENT SKILL

"Parents, if you don't teach your kids personal finance lessons, they likely will never receive any financial education. It's your responsibility to ensure they are ready to leave your home with the skills, behaviors, and systems that will help them be self-sufficient members of society and can avoid the pain associated with money struggles" Vince Shorb.

FACTS AND STATS

1. Over 53% of adults say thinking about their financial situation makes them anxious. 44% say discussing their finances is stressful.

2. A study by the National Endowment for Financial Education (NEFE) found that less than 24% of adults have a budget and stick to it.

3. Only 24% of millennials demonstrate basic financial literacy, according to a study from the National Endowment for Financial Education.

4. According to an analysis from JPMorgan Chase, a majority of families around the world don't have enough money saved in an emergency fund.

5. The sharpest decrease in financial literacy accuracy was among those aged 18 to 34, while those 55 and older showed improvement compared to previous years."

One of the few aspects of being an adult that you should really learn quickly from the experts is finances. Unfortunately, mistakes in this area can haunt you for a long time. Hence, developing personal financial management skills is paramount for job-seeking and posterity's sake.

Personal financial management skills are skills you rely on to enable you to build personal financial integrity, intelligence, management, and practices and contribute to making wise financial decisions. Building personal financial management involves self-discipline. It is the ability to constrain and discipline yourself from taking foolish financial decisions like impulse buying, purchasing above what was budgeted, and poor saving habits. Everyone wants to enjoy one level of financial freedom, but it cannot be possible when you have poor personal financial management skills. If you cannot properly manage your finance, then you will not be able to manage the finances of others.

Personal financial management involves knowing what financial practice works for you and sticking to it. For instance, if you are a person that buys things on impulse, you may need to practice not going out with your credit cards or excess cash. You simply go out with the money you need to get what you intend to buy. Employers may not consider you for the position of an accountant or treasurer when you still struggle with personal financial management. To exercise a certain level of financial independence as a fresh graduate starting your career, you need to start now to develop personal financial management skills.

Here, are a few healthy financial practices you can indulge in to develop personal financial management skills.

- **Budgeting**

One basic aspect of developing personal financial management skills is budgeting. Surprisingly, what most people do is reverse budgeting. After the money has been spent, they finally start thinking and calculating how it was spent. This is a bad financial practice. Budgeting comes down to living within your means, and most adults were never taught this. Learning budgeting is simply a matter of attracting expenses, deciding how much to spend in each area of life, and sticking to it. The reason most people run into bad debts is simply that they live beyond their budget and earnings. Make it a habit to always stick to your budget irrespective of what comes up later. Graduates with firm budgeting skills will help their organization save costs and avoid unnecessary expenses.

- **Saving and investment**

    This is another crucial financial practice in which fresh graduates must be involved. When practicing saving or investing, always practice the principle of "pay yourself first". This is a simple concept where you focus on saving and investing with the first money you receive and then live on the rest. When you decide to save first before spending, you'll always find a way to make ends meet. Making early investments in life as fresh graduates is very important if you want to enjoy financial freedom. Therefore, you are encouraged to read and take on classes on investment to better understand profitable areas in which your funds can be invested.

- **Avoiding debts**

    Building personal financial management skills involves learning how to avoid debt. Plan for things you need and want to buy. If possible save for that item until you can afford it rather than running into debt. As much as possible for fresh graduates starting their careers from scratch, avoid debt as they will crush you even before you climb the ladder to the top.

- **Always have a contingency plan**

    In developing personal financial management skills, and as you build your career, always have contingencies plans and allot money for them so you do not get stranded and get out of cash when critical issues arise.

- **Learn to keep financial records**

    Having a good record-keeping habit is essential in building personal financial management skills. Know what you spend your money for, access your financial records and bank statements, and so on to track your expenditures and to carry out evaluation occasionally to know what your money is being spent on whether they are priorities or not. Keep receipts of payments and other financial documents safe as you advance in your career.

- **Avoid impulse buying**

    In building personal financial management skills, learn to avoid impulse buying. Buy value. Do not borrow unless you can afford it, especially in cases where the borrowed item is expensive and treasured by the owner.

    Aside from the healthy personal financial practices listed above, you must also learn to pay bills and read about finance ahead of time. It will broaden your horizon on financial management and principles that work. Make it a habit to purchase without credit cards as often as possible and finally start practicing how to balance cheque books. You do not necessarily have to study financial accounting in school to be able to develop personal financial management skills. It can be learnt simply by practice.

    Graduates with very good financial management skills can be given highly placed positions in their organizations as employers are looking for people with financial integrity to recruit for accounting and other vital financial positions.

Action Point

Building personal financial management skills will not happen like a dream. It's a step at a time until you arrive at financial freedom.

21

SPEED READING SKILLS

"I read a book twice as fast as anybody else. First, I read the beginning, and then I read the ending, and then I start in the middle and read toward whatever end I like best." - **Gracie Allen**

FACTS AND STATS

1. The average reading speed for an adult is around 200 to 300 words per minute. Speed readers can read up to 1,000 words per minute or even more.
2. The world record for speed reading is held by Anne Jones, who read 4,700 words per minute with 67% comprehension.
3. Speed reading techniques can improve reading speed by up to 300%.
4. The ability to speed read is not dependent on intelligence but can be developed through practice and training.
5. A study by the University of California found that speed reading training led to an increase in reading speed by an average of 50% without a decrease in comprehension.

Reading is a fundamental skill that we use every day. From emails and social media posts to books and academic papers, we are constantly reading. However, the speed at which we read can vary greatly from person to person. Some people read at a snail's pace, while others can breeze through a book in a matter of hours. As a fresh graduate, if you find yourself in the former category, don't worry. With the right techniques, you can increase your reading speed and become a more efficient reader. In this chapter, we'll explore 15 simple techniques to help you do just that.

- **Set A Reading Goal**

Setting a reading goal for yourself is one of the most effective strategies to increase the amount of text that you can read in a given amount of time. To accomplish this, all you need to do is set a goal for yourself regarding the number of pages you want to read in a given amount of time. You might, for instance, decide that you want to read 20 pages in one hour as a target. You can provide yourself with something to work toward and assist in focusing your attention on the activity at hand by defining a goal for yourself.

- **Use a pointer**

You can speed read by using a pointer like your finger or a pen to guide your eyes while you read. You can read more efficiently if you move the pointer along the page, focusing on the text as it passes under the cursor. You may improve your reading speed and minimize the amount of time your eyes have to spend going back and forth by using this method.

- **Improve Your Focus**

Your reading speed might be slowed down by distractions, and it can become more difficult to understand what you're reading as a result. Reading in a calm setting with few interruptions can help increase your ability to focus on what you're doing. You might also try putting on some white noise or listening to some ambient music in order to help filter out any outside noises.

- **Skim and Scan**

You can read more rapidly by employing the reading strategies of skimming and scanning, which allow you to swiftly find relevant information. Skimming is the process of reading a text fast to gain a high-level understanding of its content. When you scan, you look for certain words or phrases within the text. Using these methods can be very helpful when reading lengthy documents or academic papers.

- **Use Chunking Technique**

    Reading a text in chunks requires dividing it up into sections that are both more digestible and more manageable. You might, for instance, divide a lengthy paragraph into two or three shorter paragraphs to make it easier to read. If you do this, you will be able to concentrate on each component separately, which will help you enhance both your reading comprehension and your reading speed.

- **Read With Some Energy**

    When you read actively, you interact with the material you're reading and pose questions to yourself as you go. For instance, you might ponder why the author chose to include a particular piece of information or what the primary focus of a given paragraph is. You can enhance both your comprehension and reading speed by taking an active role in interacting with the text.

- **Stop the Inner Monologue**

    Stopping the inner monologue can also improve reading speed and comprehension. When we read, our minds tend to subvocalize or mentally read each word, which slows down our reading pace. By quieting the inner monologue, we can eliminate this habit and train our brains to process words faster. To do this, try using techniques such as speed reading or scanning, which focus on visualizing the content instead of reading each word individually. For example, try using your peripheral vision to read multiple words at once instead of fixating on one word at a time.

- **Reduce Subvocalization**

To increase reading speed, it's important to reduce subvocalization - the silent pronunciation of words while reading. While this can aid comprehension, it also slows down the reading process. Instead of focusing on each word, concentrate on the overall meaning of the text. For example, instead of subvocalizing every word in a sentence, try to grasp the main idea and read at a faster pace.

- **Use Peripheral Vision**

Try reading with your side vision to read faster and with less strain. This means you should look at the middle of the page and let your side vision take in the words around it. In this way, you can read more words at once and speed up how fast you read. For example, instead of focusing on one word at a time, use your peripheral vision to read whole phrases or sentences at once.

- **Take Breaks**

It is critical to take regular breaks while reading to avoid burnout and improve reading speed. This keeps you intellectually alert and interested with the text. For example, after reading for 20 minutes or so, take a five-minute break to stretch your muscles and then return to reading with renewed attention.

- **Use of Timer Exercises**

Put your reading skills to the test by using a metronome or a timer and see how you can increase your speed with time. Just read normally for a minute. WordstoPages is a handy tool for keeping track of how many words you've read. You need to go through the steps again and write down the new total. Have a positive attitude and strive to improve with each new count. Give yourself a treat when you succeed at something each day or each week. Playing this fast game will increase your reading speed.

- **Leverage On Technology**

Technology can be a valuable resource when it comes to improving your reading speed. There are many apps and tools available that can help you read more efficiently and effectively. For example, the Spritz app allows you to read text one word at a time, at a speed of your choosing. This can help you increase your reading speed while maintaining comprehension. Similarly, the Spreeder app can help you improve your reading speed by training your eyes to move more efficiently across the page. By incorporating technology into your reading routine, you can develop better reading habits and make the most of your reading time.

- **Read Regularly**

Practice makes reading faster. Reading faster improves with practice. "Practice makes perfect" is true. Professionals — artisans, athletes, artists, musicians, etc. — practice regularly. Readers should too. Read more, get better. Reading faster increases with reading skill. Theodore Roosevelt read one book before breakfast and three or four at night. He read pamphlets and publications. These books were probably average length. Utilize his obsession as motivation.

- **Improve On Your Vocabulary**

Imagine you're in the middle of a book and you come across a word you don't know. Is it something you rush past,

PERSONAL FINANCIAL MANAGEMENT SKILL

try to guess at, or pause to look up? Every alternative slows you down or prevents you from reading altogether. The best way to fast read is to increase your vocabulary. One's reading and comprehension speeds increase in proportion to one's vocabulary size. This allows you to read more in less time. This is a crucial factor to think about when trying to improve reading abilities.

- **Don't sacrifice comprehension for speed**

When working on improving your reading speed, it's crucial to remember not to prioritize speed over comprehension. It's important to find a balance that works for you between the two. By doing so, you'll be able to read quickly while still being able to understand the material. Giving up understanding for speed can lead to misunderstandings, mistakes, and a waste of time. So, take the time to learn how to read quickly while also making sure you fully understand what you're reading.

Incorporating speed reading techniques into your daily reading habits can significantly improve your reading speed and comprehension. Practice daily with techniques like skimming, chunking, and minimizing subvocalization. Set specific goals and track your progress regularly to keep yourself motivated. Remember, consistent effort and dedication will lead to significant improvements in your reading speed and overall efficiency. As Napoleon Hill once said, "Reading is to the mind what exercise is to the body." So, get to exercising your mind and start reading!

Action Point:

As a graduate, rapid reading can boost your research, industry knowledge, and professional productivity. To improve your reading speed and comprehension, practice skimming, scanning, and limiting subvocalization. Take action immediately and get career-long reading improvements.

22

SIMPLE ETIQUETTE SKILLS

"Good manners are just a way of showing other people that we have respect for them"- Bill Kelly

FACTS AND STATS

1. A recent survey of over 2,000 workers found that 80% believe that a lack of common courtesy is a serious problem in the workplace.

2. Etiquette has become increasingly crucial in our world with 24/7 communication across multiple platforms and rapidly decreasing first impression opportunities.

3. According to a recent study, a staggering 57% of adult participants were unaware of the social etiquette that dictates that platters and bows of food should be passed to the right.

4. According to a survey, 83% of respondents indicated that they and their friends should improve their table manners.

5. 66% of college students believe that good manners and etiquette are crucial for success and that showing respect improves mental health.

Manners are the basic building blocks of civil society. Learning and practicing simple etiquette and mannerisms will help you build good social relationships with people. There are rules of engagement for every game therefore, maintaining simple etiquette rules will enable you to outclass the competition. Simple etiquette skills are the missing links between your education and success in the business world. They are people's first impression of you before they get to know you.

Maintaining simple etiquette will help you build social relationships and prepare you to function perfectly among the class of people you want to network with and get the kind of job you desire.

SIMPLE ETIQUETTE SKILLS

Here are lists of simple etiquette skills you can constantly practice to find your dream job and remain employable in the corporate world.

- Always have a prepared 60 self-introduction pitch for every interview and networking you attend. This will make people interested in you, and make you leave a lasting impression behind. It should be catchy and well-articulated. This will help you know what to say when you meet new people.

- Engage in eye contact, maintain good posture and shake hands firmly. These things speak volumes of your confidence and credibility as a person on a mission to achieve greatness. Eye contact is necessary to build boldness when you appear before people especially during interviews and presentations.

- Dress up for success. You will be addressed the way you choose to dress. Wear the right business attire that showcases the style of those in your industry or profession. Polished shoes translate to attention to detail. Ensure your shoes are neatly polished as a polished appearance can open doors.

- Be on time and stay on task. This may sound simple but it takes discipline to achieve. Delaying meetings due to tardiness or sneaking in after a meeting begins will reflect poorly on you. You should arrive at meetings two to three minutes early and be ready to follow the lead of whoever runs the meeting. Meetings usually have a specific agenda with a planned time for each topic. Don't derail the conversation with something not part of the agenda. If you have a topic that should be discussed, ask for it to be added to the agenda in advance, follow up with your question during the Q&A if time allows, or when the meeting has concluded send a note via email to the appropriate person.

- Avoid the use of slang, foul language, or filler of words. Rather cultivate a strong, clear speaking voice. Effective communication is key to successful social interactions. Learn the appropriate language of communication that will best suit your audience.

- Set a good example, be positive, and don't gossip. It's always important that feedback be constructive, especially in a group setting. If there is something you disagree with, make sure you communicate it to the right audience (which is often not the entire group). Being negative within an organization will give you a bad reputation. If you have an issue, talk directly with the person who can address your concerns. Do not get sucked into negativity and do not be the one who instigates gossip.

- Conduct yourself in a business-like manner at all times. Learn the business terms and jargon applicable in your field. Use them correctly whether in speech or written communication. People will connect with you easily when you acceptably conduct yourself.

- Always identify yourself when placing and answering a call. It is always considered professional and appropriate when using a landline and cell phone for business.

- Know that HR professionals often take their time to google your name before meeting you in person. Hence, you must know what is appropriate and does not reflect positively upon you when using your social networking tools. You make your first impression online. Do not let your prospective employers perceive you in the wrong manner.

- Make good use of your networking skills, mingling and small talk will help you get a job but will also help you stand out in your new job. Learn to engage people in meaningful conversations. It could begin with a simple how are you and what do you do.
- Always practice good dining skills and suitable table manners. Be polished and professional at the dining table. Be conscious to observe your table manners as a potential employer may schedule an interview with you over lunch.
- Practice good manners at all times. Be civil at all times whether in a social or corporate gathering. People remember people with good manners to occupy salient positions in their organization. You stand a chance if you work at developing this vital skill.

Action Point

Your ability to maintain simple etiquette at all times shows how serious and self-disciplined you are.

23

SAFETY AND SECURITY SKILLS

'Safety and security don't just happen, they are a result of collective consensus and public investment. We owe our children, the most vulnerable citizens in our society, a life free of violence and fear"- Nelson Mandela.

SAFETY AND SECURITY SKILLS

FACTS AND STATS

1. Being the victim of a home burglary can increase the risk of future victimization for burglary, as offenders often target the same residence more than once.
2. Dog ownership has been found to reduce the likelihood of burglary and other property crime.
3. About 60% of convicted burglars say the presence of an alarm would steer them to a different home to burglarize.
4. Almost 40% of young adults admitted texting or emailing at least once while driving in the past 30 days.
5. With an average of 97 cybercrime victims per hour, this means there is a victim of cybercrime every 37 seconds.

Graduating from college or university is an exciting time for most students. After years of hard work, you finally have your degree in hand, and you're ready to enter the workforce. However, as you transition into the professional world, it's important to remember that safety and security should be a top priority. This is particularly true if you're starting a job that involves working with people, handling valuable assets, or dealing with potentially dangerous situations.

Developing safety and security skills is crucial for fresh graduates who are new to the workforce. Employing safety and security skills in discharging your duties will enable you to access risk and possible safety hazards of all aspects of operations and be on the lookout for any unsafe behavior or breaks in regulations. These skills can also help you protect yourself, your colleagues, and your company from potential harm. In this chapter, we'll discuss some of the most important safety and security skills that fresh graduates should develop.

SAFETY AND SECURITY SKILLS

- **Situational Awareness**

One of the most important safety and security skills that you can develop is situational awareness. Situational awareness is the ability to perceive and understand your environment, anticipate potential threats, and take proactive measures to mitigate them. This means being aware of your surroundings and the people around you at all times.

Developing situational awareness starts with paying attention to your environment. When you're in a new place or situation, take a few moments to look around and take in your surroundings. Notice the exits, the people around you, and any potential hazards. Pay attention to your instincts, and don't ignore any red flags or warning signs.

- **The Need for Effective Communication**

Effective communication is key to maintaining a safe and secure workplace. As a fresh graduate, you'll likely be working with a team of people, and it's important to be able to communicate effectively with them. This means not only being able to speak clearly and concisely, but also being able to listen actively and ask questions when necessary.

In a crisis situation, clear and concise communication can be the difference between life and death. Make sure that you know how to communicate with your colleagues and superiors in an emergency, and practice your communication skills regularly.

- **Conflict Resolution**

In any workplace, conflicts can arise. As a fresh graduate, it's important to know how to handle conflicts in a calm and professional manner. This means being able to listen to all parties involved, understand their perspectives, and work to find a solution that satisfies everyone.

Developing conflict resolution skills can be challenging, but it's an essential part of creating a safe and secure workplace. Take the time to learn about different conflict resolution techniques and practice them regularly.

- **Self-Defense**

In some workplaces, employees may be at risk of physical harm. If you work in a high-risk environment, it's important to have basic self-defense skills. This doesn't necessarily mean learning martial arts or carrying a weapon; it means knowing how to protect yourself and others if necessary.

Consider taking a self-defense class to learn basic techniques for defending yourself. Even if you never need to use these skills, knowing that you have the ability to protect yourself can give you confidence and peace of mind.

- **Emergency Preparedness**

In an emergency, every second counts. Knowing what to do in a crisis situation can help you stay calm and take appropriate action. As a fresh graduate, it's important to understand the emergency procedures and protocols in your workplace. This means knowing where the emergency exits are, how to evacuate the building in a crisis, and how to use any emergency equipment such as fire extinguishers.

Take the time to familiarize yourself with the emergency procedures in your workplace, and practice emergency drills regularly. This will help you be prepared in the event of an emergency.

- **Cyber security**

In today's digital age, cyber security is more important than ever. As a fresh graduate, you'll likely be working with computers, networks, and other digital systems. It's important to know how to keep these systems secure and protect them from cyber-attacks.

Start by learning about the common types of cyber threats and how to recognize them. Phishing, for example, is a common tactic used by cyber criminals to steal sensitive information. By understanding what a phishing email looks like, you can avoid falling for this type of scam.

You should also understand how to create strong passwords and keep them secure. Use a combination of uppercase and lowercase letters, numbers, and special characters to create a strong password that's difficult to crack. And never share your passwords with anyone or write them down in a place where they could be easily found.

- **First Aid**

Knowing basic first aid skills can be extremely helpful in a workplace emergency. Whether it's a minor injury or a more serious medical emergency, being able to provide basic first aid can make a big difference in the outcome.

Consider taking a first aid course to learn the basics of treating injuries, administering CPR, and dealing with other medical emergencies. Even if you never need to use these skills, knowing that you have them can give you the confidence to respond effectively in an emergency.

SAFETY AND SECURITY SKILLS

- **Risk Assessment**

Risk assessment is the process of identifying potential hazards and evaluating the likelihood and severity of those hazards. This is an important skill for anyone working in a high-risk environment, but it's also important for all employees to have a basic understanding of risk assessment.

Learn how to identify potential hazards in your workplace, and think critically about how to mitigate those risks. This might mean taking proactive measures to prevent accidents, such as improving safety protocols or providing additional training for employees.

- **Time Management**

Time management might not seem like a safety or security skill at first glance, but it's actually extremely important for maintaining a safe and secure workplace. When employees are rushed, stressed, or overwhelmed, they're more likely to make mistakes or take shortcuts that could compromise safety.

By developing strong time management skills, you can ensure that you have the time and resources to complete your work safely and efficiently. This means setting realistic deadlines, prioritizing tasks, and delegating work when necessary.

- **Continuing Education**

Finally, it's important to remember that safety and security skills are not something you can learn once and forget about. As technology and workplace environments evolve, new threats and challenges will emerge. It's important to stay up-to-date with the latest safety and security practices, and to continue learning and improving your skills over time.

Consider attending workshops or conferences related to safety and security, or taking additional training courses to expand your knowledge and skills. By investing in your own education and development, you can become a more valuable employee and help create a safer and more secure workplace for everyone.

Developing safety and security skills is crucial for fresh graduates as they enter the workforce. By developing skills such as situational awareness, communication, conflict resolution, self-defense, emergency preparedness, cybersecurity, first aid, risk assessment, time management, and continuing education, you can help protect yourself, your colleagues, and your company from potential harm. These skills may not be required in every job, but they're an essential part of being a responsible and effective employee in any workplace.

Action Point

No company or organization can survive without considering the safety and security of lives and properties that's why they employ safety professionals to enable them to carry out their activities peacefully.

24

PUBLIC SPEAKING SKILLS

"There are three things to aim at in public speaking: first, to get into your subject, then to get your subject into yourself, and lastly, to get your subject into the heart of your audience." – Alexander Gregg

FACTS AND STATS

1. Your first 20 seconds matters. You only have one chance to make a good first impression and that first impression is formed within 20 seconds.
2. 100% of audiences will appreciate you as a speaker ending on time. No one appreciates a speaker who goes over time.
3. Approximately 75% of people suffer from speech anxiety, also known as Glossophobia and the average person ranks the fear of public speaking higher than the fear of death.
4. The average attention span of an adult is 20 minutes, making it important for speakers to capture and maintain their audience's attention.
5. 55% of communication is nonverbal, making body language an important aspect of public speaking. 7% is verbal which is what you say and 38 % is vocal meaning how you say it.

Public speaking is an essential skill that can have a significant impact on your personal and professional life. As a fresh graduate, you may find yourself in situations where you need to speak in front of an audience, whether it's giving a presentation at work, delivering a speech at a conference, or even making a toast at a friend's wedding.

The ability to communicate effectively and confidently is a valuable asset that can set you apart from your peers give an edge both personally and professionally. Here are seven reasons why you should learn public speaking (even if you hate it like me)

- **Build confidence:** Public speaking can help build your confidence and self-esteem. As you develop your skills, you'll feel more comfortable and at ease speaking in front of others.

- **Improve communication skills:** Public speaking requires clear and effective communication. As you work on your speaking skills, you'll also improve your ability to communicate in other areas of your life, such as in job interviews or interpersonal relationships.

- **Enhance critical thinking:** Preparing a speech requires research and critical thinking skills. You'll need to gather information, analyze it, and present it in a clear and compelling way.

- **Develop leadership skills:** Public speaking can help you develop leadership skills, as you learn to inspire and motivate others with your message.

- **Expand your network:** Speaking at events or conferences can help you connect with like-minded individuals and expand your professional network.

- **Boost your career:** Public speaking skills can be a valuable asset in the workplace, as you may be called upon to deliver presentations or communicate with clients or customers.

- **Make a difference:** Public speaking can give you a platform to share your message and make a positive impact on others. Whether it's advocating for a cause or sharing your expertise on a topic, public speaking can be a powerful tool for change.

But public speaking can be intimidating. It's natural to feel nervous or anxious before a big speech, but with the right preparation and techniques, you can develop your public speaking skills and deliver a compelling presentation that captivates your audience. In this chapter, we'll explore 17 tips on developing your public speaking skills, from preparation to delivery and everything in between.

- **Tip #1: Know Your Audience**

Before you start preparing your speech, it's crucial to understand your audience. Who are they, what do they already know, and what do they want to learn from your speech? By tailoring your message to your audience, you can ensure that your speech is relevant and engaging. The best way to connect to your audience is to pay attention to your audience's distinctiveness and complexity.

- **Tip #2: Start With a Strong Opening**

Your opening is the first impression you make on your audience, so it's essential to make it count. A strong opening can capture your audience's attention and set the tone for the rest of your speech. Consider starting with a surprising fact, empirical statistics, a thought-provoking question, or a personal anecdote that relates to your topic. The first 30 seconds and the last 30 seconds have the most impact in a presentation." – Patricia Fripp

- **Tip #3: Use Storytelling**

To connect with people, we must show them a little bit of ourselves, personalize things, and ideally imbue our stories with a genuine feeling of emotion and compassion. Consider how you may add real-life tales and stories into your presentation. That will make you much more memorable and will aid in increasing audience involvement.

- Tip #4: Practice, Practice, Practice

This may sound apparent, yet it is often overlooked: nothing beats practice for getting ready for a large presentation. If you're going to give a presentation in person, practice it out loud, in front of a mirror, or with a colleague. Even better, if you're preparing for an online presentation, set up a Zoom conference and videotape yourself speaking. Then be bold enough to look back - you'll be astonished at what you discover. Practice will help you feel more confident and comfortable with your material. "It's what you practice in private that you will be rewarded for in public." – Tony Robbins.

- Tip #5: Use Visual Aids

Visual aids can be a great way to enhance your presentation and keep your audience engaged. Consider using slides, charts, or videos to illustrate your points. For instance, here are a few examples of how you can utilize PowerPoint and Google Slides: add animations, video, audio, and create a timeline.

- Tip #6: Control Your Voice and Body Language

It is critical to learn how to utilize your voice appropriately when giving a public speech. Managing your body language is also important. Smooth breathing is a useful skill for controlling your voice. This helps to prevent shortness of breath, which can occur when one is anxious. It can also make your voice sound stronger and clearer. Your body language can communicate just as much as your words. Use confident posture, make eye contact, and use gestures to emphasize your points.

- **Tip #7: Avoid Awkward Fillers "Um," "Uh," "Like."**

Without realizing it, we all use filler words in our talks. But, using these terms excessively during a professional speech might make you appear unconfident. Break the habit of utilizing these terms if you can to improve your public speaking skills. Practicing can help you eliminate these terms from your speech patterns, but you may be so accustomed to using them that you don't realize you're doing it. Here is where a speech coach, instructor, or friend may help.

- **Tip #8: Engage With Your Audience with Questions**

Engaging your audience may help them stay interested and attentive. Consider asking questions or requesting comments, and be prepared to respond to their responses. Not only does asking questions allow you to catch your breath and organize your ideas, but it also allows you to listen and interact with your audience. A critical statistic for gauging their interest and engagement. Inquiries are also effective rapport builders since they signal the start of a relationship.

- **Tip #9: Be Authentic**

Authenticity is the cornerstone of effective public speaking. You can't be an effective public speaker unless you have it. If you reflect back on all the fantastic presentations you've seen, chances are that sincerity was what made it stay. Let your personality to show through in your speech.

- **Tip #10: Don't Read Unless You Have To. Work from an Outline.**

Reading from a script or from a slide breaks down the human connection. You retain the audience's attention on yourself and your message by keeping eye contact with them. A simple overview might help you remember things and stay on track. Complex language and technical terminology, on the other hand, may turn off your viewers. Avoid unnecessary jargons and keep your message basic and obvious.

- **Tip #11: Incorporate Some Humor**

Humor can be a great way to connect with your audience and keep them engaged. Consider incorporating a funny anecdote or joke that relates to your topic. Unless you are presenting something really serious, try adding some comedy into your presentation. This can help to lighten the tone and keep people engaged in what you're saying. Sometimes, consider telling a work-related joke to begin your presentation.

- **Tip #12: Use Repetition**

Repeating key points throughout your speech can help reinforce your message and ensure that your audience remembers your main ideas. Repetition especially when done in unison with audience can significantly hold their attention. According to John Maxwell "The first time you say something, it's heard; the second time, it's recognized; the third time, it's learned."

- **Tip #13: Volunteer to Present**

Speaking in front of a crowd is, of course, one of the finest methods to become a more confident speaker. Confidence is key to delivering a successful speech. As a fresh graduate, consider taking advantage of any opportunities to speak in your immediate environment. You will gradually gain confidence in front of your complete organization by beginning with a small crowd.

- **Tip #14: Appreciate Yourself**

Even if you are not a professional public speaker, most people will respect your willingness to speak in front of an audience. Remind yourself that every time you give a presentation, you are improving your presenting abilities. Making errors allows you to learn and develop. Remember, a professional speaker was once an amateur.

- **15: Dress For Success**

Are there dress rules? Not really. It all depends on your audience. Dress in a way that makes you feel comfortable and confident. You will feel better if you look well. The better you feel, the more assured you'll be. The more assured you are, the more probable it is that you will deliver an excellent speech.

- **Tip #16: Recap at The End**

You communicated your point to an attentive audience. You conveyed a clear, cohesive point while presenting with confidence and elegance. Yet you may be wondering, "Are they going to remember what I said?" This is an important consideration when you conclude your speech. You should conclude your speech by swiftly summarizing your main ideas. Keep in mind that you are not repeating yourself word for word. You're going through your important points again in summary style. This allows you to end on a high note.

- **Tip #17: Seek Feedback**

Seeking feedback from others can help you improve your public speaking skills. Ask a trusted friend, your manager or a colleague to evaluate your performance and provide constructive feedback. That way, you can learn what you need to improve on before and after every presentation.

Developing your public speaking skills can be challenging, but with practice and dedication, you can become a confident and effective speaker. Continuously seek opportunities to improve, whether it's attending workshops, reading books on public speaking, or watching TED Talks.

Remember to prepare thoroughly, engage with your audience, and be authentic in your delivery. With these 17 tips, you'll be well on your way to mastering the art of public speaking and making a lasting impact on your audience.

As a fresh graduate, developing your public speaking skills can set you apart in your professional life, so invest in your communication skills and watch your confidence and career soar. "Public Speaking is a skill that can be studied, polished, perfected. Not only can you get good at it, you can get damn good at it and it makes a heck of a difference." – Tom Peters.

Action Point

My sincere recommendation is to avoid starting with PowerPoint. Presenting tools compel you to go through material in a linear fashion, and you should actually begin by thinking of the entire rather than the individual lines.

25

JOB INTERVIEWING SKILLS

"Be so good they can't ignore you" Steve Martin

FACTS AND STATS

1. An average length of an interview is 45 - 90 minutes, 37% of 2020 surveyed recruiters indicated they know within the first 90 seconds if they will hire that candidate.
2. 55% of interview candidates are dropped because of the way they are dressed, acted or walked through the door.
3. 39% of the candidates leave a bad impression due to their overall confidence level, voice quality, or lack of a smile.
4. 47% of interview candidates are eliminated who had little or no knowledge of the company.
5. 60% of hiring managers use or have used video interviewing in the hiring process.

Get this straight, the stakes are high, you need to be so good not to be ignored. Don't get nervous that you make your heart thump, just relax. Depending on how you choose to start, you could win the hiring manager over from the very start of the conversation. You could also disqualify yourself even before the interview starts. This is why you must get your interviewing skills and techniques right before you go for an interview.

Here are a few tips that will help you scale through.

- **Adequately prepare and do proper research**

    Preparation is the key to success in any interview. But most fresh graduates don't prepare enough, which is why they fail. They fail to research the company they are being interviewed at. This could be very embarrassing. A fundamental rule of thumb is to research the company and also prepare your lists of questions to ask the interviewers. This will show that you are someone who spends time in getting to know their prospective future employers. You need to prove that you've done your homework to get the job. Preparation doesn't simply mean skimming through the company's Wikipedia page. You need to go out of your way to find out as much as possible about the company, its culture, the industry trends, and so on. That's how you demonstrate your worth to the interviewer.

- **Draft Stories**

Before you get to any interview draft your storylines. Your interviewer wants to see how your current skills complement the job requirements. The best way to prove them is to draft stories about your previous achievements. This is because stories are more convincing than factual data. Make sure your stories are interesting and to the point. Your opening line should be good and catchy; see to it that you've learned them by heart.

- **Give Right Answer**

Avoid being diplomatic in answering questions, give straightforward answers that are right and can be verified if the need arises. You should avoid rehearsing lines and give genuine answers to seemingly common questions.

- **Identify your unique strength and potentials**

This is your time to talk about your strengths, how you are the right fit for the job, and what you can offer them if they hire you. Being able to identify your unique strength is what will make you stand out from other candidates. Is it creativity, grit, resilience, patience, or doggedness? Talk about them and be prepared to give instances where you exhibited these strengths. Your focus should be on your potentials and not your inabilities. Like any other candidate, you too are not perfect, so you shouldn't give the interviewer a chance to discuss where you lack. Instead, lay more emphasis on your potential, which clearly shows you have what it takes to succeed at the job. Of course, as a fresh graduate, you may not have real-world experience, but you can talk about your quick learning and adapting abilities. It helps you win the confidence of your interviewer to a great extent. You might not also have highly specialized skills and years of experience under your belt, which is why you've applied for the job to start gaining experience but you do have some unique potentials to offer and that is what they should be focusing on. That's the uniqueness that you need to use to make an impact on your interviewer.

- **Know how to tackle competency-based interview questions**

    Competency-based questions are designed to check your knowledge, skills, and attitude. You may be asked how well you can handle stress or a high-pressure workplace. Giving examples of how you handled such situations will better answer competency-based questions.

- **Avoid overselling yourself**

    You should know where to strike the balance between overselling yourself and expressing your prowess. Be confident, but not arrogant. Be vocal, but not annoying. Sell your potential and your talent but don't do it excessively. Do you know how they say you should "be yourself" to make the best impression? It's advice that you should stay away from when being interviewed. While it's good to be enthusiastic, energetic, and positive during your interview - don't oversell yourself. The simple reason is that employers know that there's a lot of talent in the market. And candidates can go to any extent to get the job - even exaggerate their skills and experience. So, if you're going to say something, you better back it with solid proof.

Interviews for fresh graduates are always a difficult experience but the more prepared focused and determined you are, the better your chances of securing the job. Scaling successfully through the interview process depends on how badly you want the job and why you believe you are the right fit. Constant practice and writing down things you know about yourself, including your strengths and weaknesses, will help you a great deal. The more you know yourself, the better you will ace the interview.

Action Point

A farmer does not go to the farm without being prepared. Likewise, you cannot afford to appear before interviewers unprepared. You should be ready for a disappointment if you do.

26

STRESS MANAGEMENT SKILLS

"Stress management is life management. If you take control of your stress, your life will thank you for it"- Sheraka Dunston

FACTS AND STATS

1. Of the adults who reported feeling stressed, 51% also indicated feeling depressed, while 61% stated experiencing anxiety.

2. The workplace is a common source of stress for many people because more than 75% working class said that work was a significant source of stress.

3. Out of those who have experienced stress in their lives, 16% reported engaging in self-harm, and 32% stated having had suicidal thoughts and feelings.

4. Of those experiencing high levels of stress, 36% of women attributed it to their comfort with their appearance and body image, while only 23% of men did the same.

5. Roughly 69% of adults in the United States report feeling stressed at least once a month, with more than half of respondents reporting feeling stressed daily.

Williams James expressed his thoughts on stress management when he said" the greatest weapon against stress is our ability to choose one thought over another". I agree with this thought. Our inability to choose one thought over another is the major reason we are stressed out as we tend to do more than we can at a time. Often, we want to do a lot of things all at the same time that our body system may not be prepared for.

There is a parable of a frog sitting in a pot on the stone. If dropped into a pot of boiling water, a frog would likely notice and try to escape. However, when placed in a pot slowly approaching a boil, the frog doesn't notice until the water has already reached unbearable heat, when it is too late for the frog to survive. That is how you slowly accept pressures around you until it is so much that you can barely cope.

According to Gale Encyclopedia of Medicine 2008, stress management is a set of techniques and programs intended to help people deal more effectively with stress by analyzing the specific stressors and taking positive actions to minimize their effects.

Stress has been referred to as the 'silent killer" as it can lead to several other ailments such as heart disease, high blood pressure, chest pain, and an irregular heartbeat. This is why it is important to take good care of your health to avoid breakdown and further ailment. You need to stay fit and alive to reach the peak of your dream career, hence the need to know how to manage stress at work and all around.

The American psychological association listed 7 proven tips to help individuals develop effective stress management skills to increase productivity, especially at work. They are:

    i.   **Understand your stress**

Know how you are stressed. It can be different for everybody but understanding what stress is to you can help you better prepare before it arises.

    ii.   **Identify your stress sources**.

Know what causes you to be stressed. If it's work, family, change, or anything else. Be sure to identify it and know how to avoid it.

    iii.   **Learn to recognize stress signals**

Different individuals process stress differently so it is important to be aware of your stress symptoms. Could it be low tolerance, headaches, stomach pains, sleeplessness, weight gain or weight loss, irritability, fatigue, and the rest of them? When you can recognize these symptoms, you get better at managing stress.

    iv.   **Recognize your stress strategies**

What are your tactics for calming down? For instance, some people cope with stress by self-medicating with alcohol or overeating. Know what stress reduction strategies work for you ensure to stick to the healthy ones.

v. **Implement healthy stress management strategies**

Having known your stress management strategies. Make it a priority to implement those that are healthy and you can consistently carry them out.

vi. **Make self-care a priority**

Life has no duplicate as we often say. Hence, make self-care of utmost priority. Many people are so engrossed with their jobs and career that they fail to take adequate care of themselves. When we make time for regular checkups, we put our well-being before others. It may feel selfish, but you need to be strong and well to effectively carry out your job.

vii. **Ask for support when needed**

If you are feeling exhausted, reach out to a friend or family member you can talk to. You may want to speak with a health care professional to help you learn healthier coping strategies.

If you can develop stress management skills following the above-listed tips, you will function effectively at your workplace. S/tress management in the workplace may come in different forms such as near-impossible deadlines, demanding colleagues, or unappreciative bosses. Whichever form it comes, you must be able to apply stress management skills in dealing with it. You can successfully prevent workplace stress by combining organizational changes and individual stress management techniques. Once you've identified your stress, you can start fleshing out a plan that works best for you.

Stress isn't always bad. A little bit of stress can help you stay focused, energetic, and able to meet new challenges in the workplace. It's what keeps you on your toes during a presentation or alert to prevent accidents or costly mistakes. But in today's hectic world, the workplace too often seems like an emotional roller coaster. Long hours, tight deadlines, and ever-increasing demands can leave you worried, drained, and overwhelmed. And when stress exceeds your ability to cope, it stops being helpful and starts causing damage to your mind and body and your job satisfaction. You should also monitor your body system to know when you are gradually crossing the line.

Sometimes the best stress-reducer is simply sharing your stress with someone close to you. Having someone to talk to at that time. Talking it out and getting support and sympathy especially face-to-face can be a highly effective way of blowing off stress and regaining your sense of calm. The other person doesn't have to "fix" your problems; they just need to be a good listener. A strong network of supportive friends and family members is extremely important to managing stress in all areas of your life. On the flip side, the lonelier and more isolated you are, the greater your vulnerability to stress. Build a support system to help you manage stress and when stress is mounting at work, try to take a quick break and move away from the stressful situation. Take a stroll outside the workplace if possible. Physical movement can help you regain your balance.

When you're overly focused on work, it's easy to neglect your physical health. But you're stronger and more resilient to stress when you're supporting your health with good nutrition and exercise. Taking care of yourself cannot be overemphasized when managing stress. It doesn't require a total lifestyle overhaul. Even small things can lift your mood, increase your energy, and make you feel like you're back in the driver's seat.

Also, getting a good night's sleep is fundamental for recharging and dealing with stressful situations in the best possible way. While it varies from individual to individual, an uninterrupted sleep of approximately 8 hours is generally recommended on the exact amount of sleep needed. Improve the quality of your sleep by making healthy changes to your daytime and nightly routines. For example, go to bed and get up at the same time every day, even on weekends, be smart about what you eat and drink during the day, and make adjustments to your sleep environment.

<u>Action Point</u>

The way you value your life is how others will value it too. Do not let stress rub you off your beautiful life.

27

WORK-LIFE BALANCE SKILLS

"Balance is the key to everything. What we do, think, say, eat, feel, they all require awareness and through this awareness, we can grow"- Koi Fresco

FACTS AND STATS

1. 72% of employees consider work-life balance to be very important when looking for a new job.

2. A UK study found that two thirds of businesses that implemented a 4 day work week saw an improvement in staff productivity.

3. 63% of employees say "Bad Bosses" are the biggest reason for Poor Work-Life Balance.

4. One study shows that people who work 55 hours or more per week have a 1.3 times higher risk of stroke than those who work 40 hours.

5. 73% of remote workers said they are more productive, thanks to having a better work-life balance.

Too many people get so busy making a living that they forget to make a life. When we allow work to take precedence over everything else, we'll finally realize that we were chasing shadows in the long run. Our desire to succeed professionally can push us to set aside our well-being. It is very critical to create a harmonious work-life balance to improve our physical, emotional, and mental well-being and the importance of our careers.

Balance indeed is key in whatever we do. Work-life balance is the state of equilibrium where a person equally prioritizes the demands of one's career and personal life. Once there is no equilibrium, one will be at the mercy of the other which is not good. Like two pendulum bulbs placed on a string, if one outweighs the other, there is no balance. Increased responsibilities at work, working longer hours, increased responsibilities at home, having children are common reasons that lead to a poor work-life balance.

WORK-LIFE BALANCE SKILLS

For fresh graduates just about to begin their professional lives, now is the right time to start learning how to strike a balance between your career and your personal lives before you start climbing the ropes up and it becomes extremely difficult to make any adjustments.

Work-life balance skills are a major prerequisite for career advancement. How well you utilize this skill will show how far you will go. If you fail to develop this skill and effectively put it to use, you will destroy your career even before you start. Employers who are committed to providing environments that support work-life balance for their employees can save on costs, experience fewer cases of absenteeism and enjoy a more loyal and productive workforce said Chris Chancey, career expert and CEO of Amplio Recruiting. He further stated that work-life balance is less about dividing the hours in your day evenly between work and personal life and more about having the flexibility to get things done in your professional life while still having time and energy to enjoy your personal life. This is where efficient time management skills can be employed to make work-life profitable. Balance is a very personal thing; only you can decide the lifestyle that suits you best.

Below are few steps to take in building work-life balance skills;

- **Accept that there is no perfect work-life balance**

   Always strive for a realistic schedule, not a perfect schedule. As fresh graduates, you will need enough time at work to cope with the work ethic and operations sometimes but that shouldn't be at the detriment of other areas of your life. For some days, you might need to focus more time and energy to pursue your hobbies or spend time with your loved ones. Understand that balance is achieved over time, not in one day.

- **Get a job that you love**

    You will never be happy if you hate what you do. You do not necessarily need to love every aspect of your job but do what excites you that you don't dread getting out of bed every morning. It should be a job you are passionate about not merely enduring.

- **Make your health a priority**

    You can only work and enjoy other aspects of your life when you prioritize your health and well-being. Your overall physical, emotional and mental health should be your focus. You will not be able to pursue your career if you fall in and out of sick beds. Prioritizing your health shouldn't involve radical or extreme activities but a simple daily meditation and exercise will do. In doing that you will miss less work, and you'll be happier and more productive when you are there.

- **Practice regular escapism**

    This could be simply unplugging from the outside world from time to time. It allows you to recover from weekly stress, giving you space for other thoughts and ideas to energy. Your escapism technique could be reading a romance novel instead of checking work emails. Do not be afraid to unwind. It is critical to success and helps you feel refreshed and energized to work again. This also includes taking vacation sometimes and shutting down temporarily from anything work-related.

WORK-LIFE BALANCE SKILLS

- **Create time for yourself and your loved ones**

    Your job is important especially for starters like you but it shouldn't be your entire life. Achieving work-life balance requires deliberate actions. Hence, you must be intentional in achieving it. Plan regular time out with your friends and loved ones where you can spend quality time with them playing and catching up on all the gist you've missed. The fact that your job keeps you busy does not mean you should neglect personal relationships.

- **Set boundaries and work hours**

    When you are at work, do not get entangled with thoughts of home and family members, stay focused. In the same vein, do not bring work activities home. Discuss your work boundaries with friends and families, so they understand and respect your work limits and expectations.

- **Set goals and priorities**

    Concerning your career, health and relationships set achievable goals you are passionate about. Know what tasks are most important for achieving a healthy work-life balance and ensure that you prioritize them. Know when you are most productive at work and block that time for your most important work-related activities.

Knowing how to structure and schedule your day can increase your productivity at work, resulting in more free time to relax outside work. Fresh graduates desiring to have a successful professional and personal life must build a healthy work-life balance skill. Carefully follow the steps discussed above and you'll enjoy a profitable and productive work-life moving forward.

Lastly, achieving a healthy work-life balance requires managing our professional and personal life in sustainable ways that keep our energy flowing, our minds and bodies healthy and our whole selves happy and content. It means giving due attention to all things that enrich and fulfil us including work and career, health and fitness, family and relationships, spirituality, community service, hobbies and passions, intellectual stimulation, rest, and recreation. Don't get overwhelmed by assuming you must make big changes at once. Even if you implement only a few of the above strategies, they will have a positive and measurable impact on your life. Start with one clear goal -- then add another, and another. Achieving a healthy work-life balance is like becoming a professional athlete. It takes a concerted effort to get in shape and a continued effort to stay that way. But if you can commit yourself to this quest you will reap tremendous benefits. It is possible to have a successful professional career and a fulfilling personal life. Take control of your work. Be proactive with your time. You can achieve a balanced life.

Action Point

As much as your career is important, so is every other aspect of your life. Knowing how to strike a balance is simply the way forward.

CONCLUSION

Congratulations! As you move on to the next part of your life, I want to remind you that each of the 27 skills described in this book is important and will help you live a happier, more successful life.

But it won't be easy to get good at these skills. It will take work, dedication, and a willingness to leave your comfort zone. You might even have to fail, trip, and make mistakes. But that's all right. Failure is a part of growing up, and the lessons you learn from your mistakes will help you in the long run.

So, as you start this new journey, I want you to think about these skills. Make a plan for how to improve them, and promise to do so every day. Surround yourself with people who support and encourage you, and don't be afraid to look for mentors and role models who can help you along the way.

Remember that success is a journey, not a place you arrive at. It's not something you get right away; you have to work at it every day. So, make plans, take action, and don't be afraid to change your plans as you go. Life is full of surprises, but if you stay focused on your goals and keep working on these important skills, you'll be able to get through even the toughest situations.

As a last thought, I want to leave you with this. You have the ability to do great things. You know enough, have enough skills, and want to change the world enough to do so. So, just go out and make it happen. Be the change you want to see in the world, and never stop trying to improve yourself. You can do anything you set your mind to if you work hard, are determined, and are willing to keep learning. Again, congrats, and best wishes on your journey!

www.ingramcontent.com/pod-product-compliance
Lightning Source LLC
Chambersburg PA
CBHW031533210526
45464CB00014B/1733